Frank Talk
A Book of Channeled Wisdom

Frank Talk
A Book of Channeled Wisdom

by

Tracy Farquhar

Infinite Joy Publishing,

P. O. Box 57973,

Murray, Utah 84157

http://www.spiritlightservices.com

Grateful Acknowledgment is made to the following people for helping bring this work to light.

Cover art by Shiya Stone

Cover photography by Chris Hartline

Cover design by Jonathan Benjamin

Back cover photograph by Mary Jo Rakowski

Edited and published by April Joy Rain

Printed in the United States of America

First Edition

Dedicated to Gemma and Kate,
the brightest lights on my path.

Table of Contents

Introduction

"You are an aperture through which the universe is looking at and exploring itself." — Alan W. Watts

I am a professional psychic medium and teacher with a business called Spirit Light Services. I perform intuitive life path readings using tarot cards and I connect with spirit in mediumship gatherings known as Spirit Galleries. I also teach Psychic Development classes and I am a Certified Trainer of a Law of Attraction program called Infinite Possibilities.

I began my journey to discovering my intuitive abilities in 2005 when I took classes in Psychic Development with Tom Halliwell at a local Community College. In these classes, I found that my practice readings were often quite accurate, and I found that I was picking up on the energy of spirit. As I worked with my abilities, they grew, and after lots of practice and study, I became a professional. Until recently, channeling was not a skill I had practiced very much.

In December of 2009, my sister Genie Bramlett and I were first contacted by a spirit collective who identified themselves only as Frank. This is how that initial contact came about. Genie was visiting me in New Jersey from her home state of Arizona for the Christmas holiday.

In the early morning (around 5 AM) of December 28, 2009, Genie was woken up by an unseen hand pulling sharply on her nose! She then heard a very clear voice speaking a 4-syllable name that she could not make out. The computer (which is in the room she slept in) was on, so she thought the voice might be something coming from the computer. But that didn't seem likely.

Two days before, on December 26, Genie had felt compelled to make a Ouija board out of cardboard. We used it and contacted our mom and sister Allene. We also contacted what seemed to be a spirit group called Frank. After Genie's early morning incident, we decided to ask the Ouija board what it was all about.

Q – What was the nose pulling all about?
A – *Precursor to contact. Need to clear out (mind). It is voice of real sending gentle warning.*

Q – Of what?
A – *Contact. Here for sister to further step up contact.*

Q – Was the owl Tracy heard on Christmas Eve also a gentle warning? (My daughter Kate and I both heard an owl sound outside between 3 and 3:30 AM on Christmas Eve night.)
A – *Yes. Tracy to use direct writing.*

Q – What should I do?
A – *Sit still. Ask us to speak. We will give further instructions. 5 PM.*

Q – Any other preparations we should do for this?
A – *Candle only. The warm light draws us.*

Shortly after 5 PM, we lit some candles and I sat with a notebook and pen. This is what I got:

Where is the long black shadow of the moon? Come to the long day. What time is it? Take the time to clear your mind. Come forward. Do you want to know how to proceed? We are here to comfort you.

We are a group of travelers who only come to those who explore consciousness on its highest level and bring light to all things. There is a tidal shift in the nodes of living beings on your planet.

We come exploring elevated consciousness as it pertains to those who are in the light. We only wish to remain for those who live the highest laws of relative humanity and endeavor to accelerate the evolution of advanced souls.

Take a break.

(I didn't go back to the writing that night.)

Around 5 PM on December 31, I tried again.

Q – Hello. Are you there?
A – *Yes, we have been waiting. Take your time and relax. We are happy you have decided to try this again. Today we will discuss the ways we can bring harmony to (here I can't read my writing).*
We have been studying you and the way you utilize your heart to employ meaning to all interactions. It is interesting to watch your process and we can see that it is not always easy to put yourself in the position of someone who imparts trust and love when others do not do the same. We can help you find the right moment to proceed with

your plans and take charge of the highest light to employ love for your highest cause.

Q – Is it my goal to publish your words?
A – *We are deciding whether to present our teachings to a wider audience. For now, you should try our suggested process to help bring more peace to your life. Keep records and do not forget to review our words. Others may find this difficult.*

Q – Should I do this daily?
A – *We would like to continue at least weekly. This is a good time for us. We are drawn to the soft twilight hours.*

Q – Did you give us a sign today?
A – *We gave a mental signal.*

Q – What is the meaning of the stars on my window? (There are two perfect 5-pointed stars on my kitchen window which look as though they were drawn by someone's wet finger. Everyone in my house says they didn't do it.)
A – *These are in your line of sight to remind you to stay connected to a higher purpose. Celestial love.*

Q – How is Genie involved in this contact?
A – *There is a lineage in your family with a history of visitations and sensitivity. We have been in contact with many of them. Gene has known us since she was a child. Tomorrow she will receive a message of confirmation that all was done for a purpose.*

Q – How will she get this message?

A – *The words will come from another in a non-threatening way. She will hear something that will resonate with her thoughts and experiences. All is well – no fear.*

Q – What do you mean by "purpose"?

A – *Purposeful action is that which resonates with the highest emotional vibration. Purpose is the (illegible) your own higher vibration and moves you forward to a higher state of being. The path you both follow takes you through a more purposeful life, therefore. You will find that we can . . .*

(At this point, Gene was in the spare room. There was a bookshelf full of books which she had previously mentioned to me was leaning as though it might fall. Right at this moment, although she didn't touch it, it fell, narrowly missing her and raining books down on the bed she slept in during her stay. If it had fallen during the night while she was asleep, she would surely have been injured.)

Q – Was there a message in the falling bookcase?

A – *Our intention was to show you that all is well and no harm will come to you. Words will not harm.*

Q – Is that all for now?

A – *Today we want you to know that your life is precious like a jewel and that we view you as faceted jewels. Your planet is most precious and we honor you. Continue to work with light, love and understanding and we will be there along with you. Try again tomorrow and listen to all words that come to you tomorrow.*

Q – Goodbye for now?
A – *Yes. Today is done.*

Around 5 PM on January 1, 2010

Q – Hello. Are you there?
A – *We were waiting for you.*

Q – I need to write more legibly. Did we receive any messages today? (We had been to see the movie Up in the Air.)

(There was a pause, then . . .)

A – *We are talking.*

(Pause)

A – *There was a message in the words you heard. Life's purpose was depicted.*

(I'm feeling some kind of interference in the connection.)

A – *Today the planetary alignment is creating a heavy atmosphere.*

Q – How many are you?
A – *8*

Q – What name should I use for you?
A – *Frank*

Q – Where are you from?

A – *The Macelonix Galaxy. We are 3.6 billion light years away.*

Q – Why are you here now?
A – *We have evolved a method of soul transference which allows us to enter wormholes astrally and visit other worlds. Our energy is comparable to that of a wave or particle traveling from one point to another. It is thought oriented. We can transfer our energy to other dimensions through controlled thought and meditation.*

Q – Why are you contacting me?
A – *You have great potential that is untapped and control can be learned to transfer your energy to achieve your highest goals.*
Take a break.

Several more automatic writing sessions were held between January 4 and 16, but after that, attempts were sporadic. I often had the feeling that I would be hearing from them again, and in April of 2013, I began the automatic writing again, and Frank let me know they wanted to write a book.

Chapter One ~ How it Began

We are a group of entities which we identify as Frank. This is the name we have chosen to call ourselves to make it easier for those we communicate with to identify us. It is not the name we normally use. We are a group of eight entities or beings from another galaxy. We communicate with you in spirit form, but we are not spirit as you would normally identify it. We are living entities who can project their consciousness through wormholes in the universe to communicate with other worlds. We do this with the intention to help and serve, and we look for those who are open to such communication through a sensitivity to energy and a willingness to connect. The open channel we are dictating this book to, Tracy, is an excellent channel and we have been with her for several years. Although she sometimes doubts her abilities, she is quite a remarkable medium and we are very pleased that she is willing to assist with the writing of this book.

We are from a galaxy far outside your solar system, 3.8 billion light years away, in a system we call the Macelonix galaxy. This is not a known area to your astronomers, as it is in the far reaches of the Universe. We are beings unlike any you have ever encountered or imagined, and although we have not transitioned to spirit through death, we are able to project the spirit energy of our material existence through space to your planet to connect and communicate with you. This has been something we have been experimenting with for many years, and only in the last couple years has this been accomplished in a clear and deliberate fashion.

We are still existing in a physical sense in our home, still conscious and living quite creative lives, while projecting part of our consciousness through the reaches of space and to your galaxy so that we may connect with you.

This concept is quite foreign to you, no doubt, as you believe that you are of one consciousness, one mind, one body and one life in your current state of existence, but we are here to tell you that this is not the case, and that you also live many different dimensional lives in various part of the universe. These lives exist in different dimensional spaces from the one you now occupy in this particular life, but these multiple lives together create the full life experience that you have chosen to incarnate into at this particular time.

The existence we experience in our world is unlike anything you experience here, but we share many similarities in our emotional and spiritual construction. There is much love among us, as there is among you, and it is at the core of our existence. This was not always the case, and it took many millennia to reach this state of grace and the acceptance of all. This love is what drives us to want to help others throughout the universe who struggle with the concepts of love, peace and universal acceptance and pure consciousness.

In the days before we transcended the struggles inherent with the material world, our system suffered many of the same complications that plague your planet. War, disease, crime and institutional corruption ran rampant, and the future of our system appeared extremely bleak for quite a long while. In the meantime, there were many advances made in the scientific study of the correlation between the mind and the soul, and between the intellect and the consciousness which, it was discovered, is quite separate from thought. It was proven that consciousness, the spirit, the soul, were quite unique energetic components of life, and that these elements were able to be separated from the physical body and the mind in such a way that they could travel through space and time without affecting the existence of the physical life left behind. And so, there is another realm of your consciousness which is living a quite different type of life in another dimensional space. This life feels and seems just as real as this life does, and in fact, it is just as real, and that is the way you experience it. But you should also know that in the dream state, these dream experiences also feel just as real and tangible as waking experiences, and so the question could be, which of my life experiences are real and which are not? Our contention is that they are all real, even the dream experiences, as they all affect your psyche and create the best atmosphere for learning, growth and ascension.

In this life, you have chosen to experience life on earth, which is a richly full and exuberant planet filled with beauty, kindness, love and many challenges. It is through your challenges and deepest despair that the greatest opportunities for growth live, and so remember that this brief time in this dimensional space is all for your highest good, and that you simply can't get it wrong, no matter what choices you make.

The lives that we continue to experience share some components with the lives you experience here, although many of the day to day stresses and worries no longer plague us. We have eliminated the need for currency and exchange as a means of survival, and so there are no longer issues of poverty and crime related to it. We have also eliminated the need for political hierarchy and oligarchy, and there is a system in place now which means we no longer need to have a single ruler or leader. In this system, many groups combine to monitor the systems in place with the intention of looking for ways to improve and expand the ways we offer services and training to the general public. The organized educational system does not exist anymore in our world, but as education is seen as a life-sustaining asset, it is quite voluntary and yet quite valuable for everyone to have equal access to it.

The idea of spirit energy is one which elicits much controversy, and we want you to know that spirit is simply conscious energy. It is the energy of the being which is housed in the physical body, and it is transmutable and infinite. It is what is at the core of all conscious beings, and it is ever-present.

We come to you as consciousness in its pure, spirit form. You often think of spirit as only accessible once the physical body is deceased, but this is not always the case. We are able to transport our spirit energy through space to various ports of call in the universe. This does not in any way diminish the spirit energy which lives within the physical existence on our home planet. We are quite alive and well, living lives which to us are quite ordinary. This part of us which is communicating with you represents just a small portion of what we really are.

Such is the nature of all conscious life. Your consciousness exists in many different states at any given time, and as a fully complete soul being, you are learning and growing in many different transfigurations of your being. The energy which constitutes your soul being is unlimited and infinite, and it exists in various states of being, both in physical reality and in spirit. And as such, the transition of your spirit from the physical at the time of death is not really a death at all, but merely a transfer of your energy to its natural state. The mourning at the death of an individual is not misplaced, and represents the sense of loss and the physical separation of our loved ones, but it is important that you realize that there is no end to our existence as spirit beings, and that the love you experienced in physical reality lives on in a state of reality that is far more real than you may imagine. Love is at the core of our spirit beings, and so the love that you share in the physical lives on in a very real way in the spiritual realms.

Here, you feel that life is transitory, and that your current state of consciousness constitutes all there is of your reality. However, this life, while quite sacred and precious, is merely a small part of your soul's experience in the existence of its infinite path. You will pass through many forms of existence as you transmute between physical and spiritual existence. This does not in any way negate the importance of this life's experience to the growth and transcendence of your soul being. Every form of existence is vitally important and sacred to the soul.

We have come to you through the channels of time and space to help you understand the nature of your existence as your world experiences a shift of consciousness that is unprecedented in its scope. There are great energetic shifts occurring in your atmosphere which are affecting many on a deeply personal level, changing their ideas of the real nature of their existence and leaving many with questions and a desire to understand more about what their purpose is in the context of the universe. Even those who appear to be skeptical about anything that cannot be proven in a scientific way are having deep energetic shifts in their field of conscious thinking, causing them to wonder about those things they have scoffed at previously. There are so many unknowns in your realm of existence; is it not possible that these unknowns are what allow you to choose your own beliefs and honor your ability to discern reality with your inner senses and intuition? This is where your true free will lies, in the realm of the unknown. It is in these choices of belief that you experience the greatest challenges of thinking and the greatest opportunity to exercise your inner knowing.

The light on our planet is very bright, as the star which provides it is closer than your sun, and so this creates a brightness to our days which is difficult to explain. This light is experienced as an aspect of the divine, and as such, it can be seen to be like a baptism of sorts when it is very strong. There are many who find it quite beautiful, and our physical reality is sustainable through the resultant heat and light, unlike yours. We woship the divine nature of the light much as some of you worship your God although we do not have anything like your organized religion. To us, all of life is evidence of the divine nature of the Universe and we find great love and comfort in the aspects of our world which are related to the creator.

There are times in our cycle when we are plunged into darkness, but these times are not of the same frequency as yours, and it is during these times that we have great celebrations to represent the bringing of the light. These celebrations honor our ability to bring light into our lives when all around us is at its darkest, and it is a way that we honor the supreme power of creation that lives within us. These periods of darkness have always been seen as sacred times and we find great joy in the lack of light, and our ability to light what appears to be empty.

Children in our society are raised by extended families including the siblings of the parents and the grandparents, who all share equally in the care and guidance of their children. They are taught independence and self-sufficiency early in life, so that they can have the courage and strength to survive our somewhat harsh conditions as well as the sometimes difficult personalities they may face as they grow older. There is always a great celebration when a child comes of age and sets out on his own. Children often make long journeys at various times in their lives before they reach maturity, so that they can learn to survive on their own and experience different life situations in different locations.

The onset of telecommunication has created broad-ranging cultural shifts and our technology, while quite different from yours, has created much of the same advances in the fields of education, commerce and social communication. It was once a fad as it is on your planet, but now it is used much more wisely, at differing times of day for some people who wish to entertain themselves with various components of the airwaves.

Our homes are mostly built underground, which assists in cooling and heating them and protecting them from the elements. Some parts of the homes will remain above ground, but the main living areas will be shielded from the bright light and will be safe and secure during some particularly strong storms which pass through at various times of the year. Some of these storms are dust storms, which can reduce visibility to zero and help us the isolate ourselves, since travel outside is restricted until the storms abate.

We have quite a lot of live theatrical performances, similar to what you have, but they are open-air performances in which the general public is invited to join in and take part. These performances can run for several days, with various actors and people from the audience stepping forth to continue the action until it is time to end it. There is great hilarity in these shows, and it is a good way to bring our people together and to relax and have fun.

Most of our food is grown in vast covered plots, and some of the growth occurs underground. We also collect water from underground springs and we have discovered many underground bodies of water which ebb and flow just as your vast waterways on Earth. We do not have such vast spaces of water, but there are small ponds and lakes which occasionally appear, but then dry up. We are never without enough water, though, as the Universe always provides.

There are many of us who do not live in traditional family roles, and it is not unusual for extended families to share housing and live in a group setting with shared responsibilities for meals and childcare. This type of group living serves us very well, as all share the daily chores so that no one person has to spend off their time doing the routine necessities and can better spend their time on other pursuits. This type of time management ensures that all have equal time to spend on learning and socializing, as well as self-care, and that the necessary chores are still managed. No one is exempt from the care of the home, children and meal preparation.

The idea of food is not the same as what you experience, as we are entirely plant-based and we do not consume any animal products at all. There are certain phyto proteins derived from an algae-like substance which is often dried and powdered and used to create a bread-like food and also used as a thickener and flavoring agent. This is a highly concentrated nutritious agent which is one of the staples of our diet. There is also a hardy crop of red grain which can be made into a paste and cooked like a cake or bread, and left to ferment for an interesting drink or beverage.

While we are still dependent on the ingestion of nutrition for energy, there is also quite a bit of energy to be derived from the ample light which bathes our planet from our star. There are times when this light is too intense to be directly experienced, but at other times, we are encouraged to spend time in the light as much nutrition and energy is derived from it.

That is all for tonight, as you need to rest. We will be with you throughout your journey and will attempt communication at some point during your event. We bid you pleasant dreams and a safe and smooth journey.

There is an awareness of self that we have developed through much study and practice which has transformed the way we handle crisis and disagreements. It is an awareness of the true nature of ourselves which now overrides the need to be right, or the need to be the one with the correct and only truth. This awareness involves the nature of connection between all beings and this can only be felt and experienced when the mind is at peace and the ego is not in a mode of self-protection. As one works with the higher spiritual aspects of the personality and sense of identity, the ego and intellect are not quite as predominant, thus allowing the soul to provide a clearer view of the situation through intuition and inner knowing. If there is an awareness of the fact that we are all one, the responses to conflict often will not be based on the need to prove that anyone is right or wrong, and will instead provide a different viewpoint of the situation with the intention of helping the other to seriously consider our situation.

This has caused personal relationships to become more integrated and important to our daily lives, but while still maintaining a strong sense of self and the divine nature of our beings which is essential to the whole. It has created a real balance between mind and body, soul and brain, intellect and emotion. It is here that we are able to function at our peak performance, even while projecting part of our spirit self through a wormhole in space to connect with you. There are great breakthroughs occurring on our planet, and so this will be our swan song for now.

There is also an awareness of the integrated nature of the various components of the soul body and how they work together to form a whole and complete sense of self. The love that we feel for ourselves when we are unable to project ourselves farther than the front porch, is extraordinary. True unconditional love occurs when the heart is aligned with the soul, and true self-love is not contingent upon our successes or failures, our appearance or our ability to attract others. It is an expression of the divine, and it is the basis of all the acts and decisions we make.

There were many adjustments we made to our society as we stressed the importance of unconditional love in all aspects of life, and it was not always easy to get everyone aligned with this new way of thinking. While we did not have the same type of religious zealots that you have, there were many who had their own belief systems which were not conducive to this type of change and so our recommendations would often fall upon deaf ears. But as tangible results were revealed through this intensive work, many others would join in this group transmutation toward unconditional love as the center of all our actions, they found that this instilled great happiness and freedom which they had never experienced before.

There was quite a lot of chaos and a sense of revolution when the government systems fell, but this was quickly abated as new systems developed and were firmly put into place. As others learned that the coup was not self-serving, and that the new system truly operated for the good of all, they came to see that this type of heart-centered leadership would be exactly right for our planet and its inhabitants.

A similar type of transition is now occurring in your own government systems, although this is not something that you're aware of.

In light of the revolutions that occurred in our systems of government, there were many shifts in the seats of power throughout the systems which previously had been the seat of influence. When business structures failed and various types of hierarchy disbanded, the monetary systems were dropped and new systems of commerce emerged which favored barter and many free services such as health care and education. Without a monetary system, there was no more corruption and poverty to be dealt with, and so many of the legal systems and systems of detention and punishment were drastically cut back. Crime is very rare now, and is usually dealt with by finding treatment for the actor as it is an indication of imbalance and need.

One of the greatest discoveries of recent times on our planet is that of a mined type of quartz crystal which has energetic powers unlike anything we have ever before experienced. These energies have been very beneficial to our systems of technology and transport, as they emit their own power which has been harnessed as an inexhaustible source of energy and is used to power many different types of transport and home systems. These crystals are found in only a few areas of our planet and were stumbled upon completely be accident by explorers who were investigating subterranean forms of life. It was found that some species of cave dwelling creatures, similar to your crustaceans, were surviving on very little nutritional sustenance other than the energy of these crystals, and so they were studied and examined for their unusual energetic emissions.

With this new energy source, we have been able to eliminate the need for most types of fuel and no longer rely on natural resources which can deplete the conditions of our planet. We have found numerous ways to utilize these crystals and there are still many different aspects of this resource which we are currently researching. It is not unlikely that a similar type of energy source exists on your planet.

It is important that you understand that your use of fossil fuels is not a permanent solution to your energy needs. While the harnessing of this type of energy has caused great strides in the development of your civilization, its usefulness has reached its peak and it is important to be open to new and cleaner sources of energy which do not cause the degradation of your environment and which do not influence the financial stability of your economy. Those who wield power will always find a reason to continue the use of exploitable resources. Remember that this is often done out of a need for control and greed. These systems cannot help but fail in the long run, but we are quite certain that your technology has already advanced beyond the need for these systems and that it is only a matter of time before the public demands the use of systems which were discovered and experimented with long ago, but which were deemed unsuitable by those in power. As the power structures disintegrate, so will the need to exploit your natural resources and the people of your planet.

We estimate through our research that our civilization began approximately 4.2 million star years ago (our years equal about 1.3 of yours). This predates your human civilization by many thousands of years, and so what seems like advances in our way of life are simply the evolution of culture and technology, and the dissolution of those systems which no longer serve their purpose. Such is the evolution of life; old systems always need to die out to make room for the new. It seems to be the nature of civilized beings, however, to resist change and so these changes often have many dissenters and sometimes must be forced upon the people who fear change.

Through our scientific, cultural and spiritual advancements, we have discovered a way to exist as one with our planet, and to honor it as though it were a living, conscious being, as many of us believe it is. We have learned that treating all conscious beings with respect and care yields much better results than violence and detention, and that loving assistance always goes farther than forcing one to conform to societal structures. These lessons were only learned after many different types of systems were shown to be ineffective and failed, leaving researchers with the task of finding those systems which worked in accordance with the laws of nature and not against them. A plant will not grow without the proper care and nutrients. How can a conscious being be expected to flourish in a system that offers little care and support outside the nuclear family? This is where we discovered the greatest results with treating those who were habitual offenders. Through loving kindness, psychological treatment and a redirection of energy, these offenders were able to be rehabilitated in the vast majority of cases. Those who were not were taken into permanent care in a loving and gentle environment rather than a prison structure.

There are many systems in place on your planet that are similar to those we once followed on ours. It is not unusual for corporate and government entities to resist any type of change which will threaten them, and so there will be great upheaval on your planet for several decades while ruling systems fail and new orders are put into place. Imagine your world in the best possible light as these transitions occur, and believe that each of you can alter the course your planet is on through your belief in the power of change which is dictated by highest order of the heart. This will ensure that it will be so, and that through great chaos comes the greatest order.

We look at you as our civilization in its early stages of infancy, and we have so much love for you. Know that all of the information dictated for the purposes of this book is given with the highest intention to help, love and serve. We have no other motivation to visit and communicate with you than to serve and assist in your planet's evolution.

Chapter Two ~ In the Highest Good

We continue to dictate this book through the medium Tracy and as our mouthpiece, Tracy is a very important part of the writing process. You may find a similar time in your life when you must trust in the integrity of another to handle a very delicate and intricate matter for you. We are very pleased that our intuition regarding Tracy has led to this point, as she is an excellent channel for our purposes, and she shares our values.

As we move onward toward a discussion of the nature of reality, it is important to realize that all of reality only exists in the NOW moment. Anything other than this exact present moment does not exist. We create each second of existence through our perceptions, emotions and self- image. There is much to be said for the power of the mind and the energy of the soul in creating the image of reality, for that is what it is, an image.

Understand that this does not in any way negate the importance of your reality in this moment in time, as all moments are precious and hold within them the divine promise of the highest form of evolution of the soul through emotional growth and deep soul learning. There is never a moment which does not hold this possibility, even those which appear to be the most mundane.

Therefore, it is important to view each moment as the most precious gift, allowing you the experience of this existence in this dimension and on this planet within the Milky Way and under the star which gives you life. This is nothing short of a miracle, and often it is quite taken for granted and the blessings are ignored. The true seat of happiness lies in the integration of this aspect of life's experiences as the supreme blessing a soul can experience, and that every emotion is precious and blessed.

We are aware of many spiritual masters who help to guide us on our paths and help to lead us through difficult twists and turns. They encourage us when we are feeling stuck and they are always there to help us with motivation and emotional support. These beings are part of your family of souls who congregate in the realm of spirit and assist you with the decisions of incarnation and the challenges in the path that you choose. They will always support your connection to your authentic self, and will encourage the expression of your divinity through your work and creative ventures in this lifetime. It is always essential to find ways to express this creativity and honor your divine light, as these are gifts which are meant to be shared with the world to inspire others to create their own lives. There is no gift which is bestowed upon someone by mistake, or which has the danger of leading someone down a wrong path. These gifts have many properties which can assist in the learning of practical life skills and decision-making. If you are true to yourself and express your creative nature, you are exercising the free will of your thoughts and your ability to move beyond any self-doubts and fears which may threaten to stop you from utilizing these gifts. It is always a good idea to honor the gifts you are born with, and learn to cultivate some of those you do not find come so easily.

As we examine the topic of free will, we acknowledge that many see conflict as a blockage to their ability to focus on the miracles of their lives and thus secure the feelings of happiness and success. We understand that any conflict, either with others or with oneself, can cause one to feel a victim of the subsequent emotions of frustration, anger and displeasure with the opposing party's unwillingness to change. Understand that it is this frustration which creates the emotions, and not the opposing party. When one is being plagued with the emotions borne of conflict, it is the feeling of helplessness and self-righteousness which cause the disquietude. When one is able to step back from the conflict and view it from a wider perspective, one has a better opportunity to see that we do not have to agree in order to feel compassion and brotherhood. There are many ways of seeing the world and many beliefs which help people to feel more comfortable with their place here; no one belief system or system of creating reality is right or wrong. When we are willing to shed the need to be correct, we then eliminate the need for this type of conflict and there is much peace to be gained by allowing opposing beliefs be.

Another type of conflict which can cause a detour on the road to happiness is grief as the result of loss. This grief can be experienced through the death of a loved one or the separation of a relationship. First, it is important that you realize the all emotions are sacred and blessed as they are expression of the deepest part of your soul. When one is experiencing what you would term a negative emotion, it is your knee-jerk reaction to want to be rid of that emotion as quickly as possible so that you can go back to feeling good, through whatever mode of living that is best achieved. But by avoiding negative emotions, we are depriving ourselves of the deep personal insight that can be obtained through them. When you experience grief, you will often describe it as "losing a part of yourself." This affords you an excellent opportunity to examine why you would have invested a part of yourself so deeply in something that is transient. Is not this life transient? Is not the Earth and the Universe transient? Does the temporary nature of anything in life make it any less sacred and divine? Do we only invest our love and our hearts in those things that we think are permanent and/or long-lasting?

These are vital questions to ask when one is evaluating the worth of one's life experiences. Much weight is placed on those experiences which are long-lasting or so-called permanent, but not much is placed on the chance meeting, the short-term relationship, the temporary job, or even the brief life. We would like to emphasize to you that every moment of your life is a sacred journey, and every relationship has its place on that journey, no matter how long or short that relationship is. Is the life of one who lives to a very old age more valuable than that of the still-born baby? It is unlikely that you would say so, but you would be quick to call a short term relationship a waste of time or useless. This is not the case, as each and every person and situation that you are blessed with offers limitless potential for growth and understanding.

This brings us the issue of failure. We often look upon relationships that do not last, either in a romantic way or as a friendship, as a failure. We see projects that do not pan out as failures, and we will accept that moniker if we feel we have failed in any way. We want you to know that this idea of failure is a falsehood, and only serves to damage one's self-worth and block one's motivation to continue to try new things and take future risks. There is no failure; the idea is merely one you have constructed in your mind to define the feeling of frustration that ensues when your expectations are not met. The key here, then, is to alter your expectations. When one brings one's attention back into the present moment and appreciates that every encounter is a blessing, one's expectations for the future of that encounter will lessen their grip, thus allowing us the free will to appreciate and acknowledge the importance of every pursuit, be it a long or short term one.

As we have stated, it has taken us many thousands of years to understand many of the concepts we are outlining in this book. It was only through trial and error that we came to understand the real nature of reality and the role that our thoughts and our view of the universe affected the way we perceive reality and how our habits can create stasis which can prevent us from proceeding along our path. As we began to take more risks with our thinking and created change in the way things were habitually being done, we were finally able to see how the world we perceive could change with our intentions. It was only when we realized that we were creating the extinction of our species through destructive and narrow-minded thinking that we found the resources to investigate other means of survival and a new system of cultural structure that would best support our growth and evolution. The subsequent expansion of our culture has been exponential.

There has never been a more fruitful time in our history; there have been so many advances in science, the arts, education and medical research since we made the many energetic and system changes in our society, that we barely recognize our home compared to what it looked like just a decade ago.

You must understand that resisting change is a natural response when we are hard-wired into habitual thinking. Even when we can see the merits of change, it is difficult to break the old habits which create a sense of comfort and safety for us. Many will voice displeasure over any type of change, and see it as negative and harmful. It is only when the change becomes the new habit that it is culturally acceptable and no longer derided. There has never been a time in the history of human culture, and in our own culture, that this has not been so. It is only those who are brave enough to face the naysayers that any kind of meaningful change will take place in the systems and structure of society.

It is because of this that we feel the need to support and encourage you through the energetic changes that are occurring on your planet, as it is these shifts which will inaugurate the need for changes in your political, social and economic structures world-wide. It simply will not be possible for your world to continue to operate under the old structures for much longer with the types of shifts that are occurring right now. These changes are already occurring in your governments and leadership, and in the corporate structures which have reached their absolute peak of growth and stability. It is essential for some of these systems to fail, in order to make room for new structures which will create more of a balanced system among the people of your planet. The wide disparities in economic and social structures need to be balanced and healed in order for your social systems to thrive. This is creating fear among those who hold the vast majority of the world's wealth as they feel their grip on this wealth and power slipping away. This will create a huge backlash which will threaten the viability of the new-found systems; however, those on the cutting edge of these new systems will be stalwart and resilient in their efforts to create lasting change which is designed to heal the planet and help it to flourish.

In the years to come, you will find many challenges to the current order which will be debated and resisted on many levels, but as the systems fall, it will become easier to implement these new structures and as people become used to the new systems and recognize their value, fewer dissenters will come forward. This is the way things proceeded in our world, and there were times when we genuinely feared for the future of our planet, such was the violence of the revolts. However, they were short-lived, and peace has now prevailed for many millennia. We feel this is similar to what is in store for you.

As the energetic shifts continue, many will be called to step forward into their power, and acknowledge their intuitive and creative talents. There will be a great need for these forward-thinking people who will become the reluctant leaders of the revolution for world-wide change. Therefore, it is important to cultivate the minds of your youth to be creative, independent and forward-thinking, and to motivate children to think outside of the proverbial box which is foist upon them with institutionalized educational systems. More and more, children are being born with a higher connection to their true soul selves, and these children will refuse to be restricted by the old boundaries of an antiquated society. As these children grow, they will be the ones who instigate great change which will be led by the calling of their hearts.

This is what we have come forward to say; this world of yours is resilient and strong, just like its people, but without a balance of energy, the future of your world would not be so encouraging. Change is necessary and coveted by those who are feeling stuck at this time. It is most important that you all follow your own intuition to find the personal changes which will best suit your path at this particular time.

We are confident that with the intelligence and compassionate hearts we have witnessed among the vast majority of your people, there is great potential for the imminent massive change which will match the energetic shifts pulling your people deeper into their soul selves and causing them to connect to themselves and each other on a higher level. You will find now that time appears to be greatly speeded up, and that your attention is often pulled away from those things which appear to be mundane or too focused on the negative. This is because you are being called to a higher duty, that of a truth-seeker and lightworker for the good of the planet and all its inhabitants. It only takes a small percentage of the population to instigate change. Do not be discouraged by the seeming power of those in charge. This will soon topple, and it will be leaders like you who are the ones to move forward with real courage and determination.

There is a great sense of balance overtaking the energy surrounding your planet right now. This means that although there are massive extinctions taking place in your animal populations, there are also great discoveries of new species and new, previously unknown species arising. It means that although vast areas of your land are being developed for human use, there are also vast areas of land which are either being reclaimed by the earth, or that are being returned to their natural state and protected. For every loss, there will be many discoveries, and for every system that falls, several new systems will take their place. Look for great strides to be made in science and medicine as these shifts occur, since the elimination of some restrictive systems will allow previously unnoticed discoveries to be made public and new research will lead to tremendously accelerated research and development.

This is a time for free thinkers, radical innovators, and creative artists to have their day in the sun. It is so vastly important that everyone begin to really focus on their own unique talents, on what they feel called to contribute to the world, and to go forward with a clear intention of love, service and self-improvement. This is what will ultimately change your world. And it is already occurring. Look around you and you'll see what we mean.

Here in our world, we have often had many reasons to despair and lose hope, and there were times when we felt we were doomed to lose everything we loved and had built for so much time. But as we began to see the progress that was being made in building new systems to replace those that were failing, we had renewed hope and energy to continue our progress toward the future. And as we continued our forward motion, we realized that it was the power of our imagination that created the new ways of being for ourselves. If it weren't for our forward-thinking vision, we would have stayed in the midst of a collapsed world with no hope and no motivation to start again. Our civilization would have died out, leaving a stark and barren landscape. It is only through the love of our planet and each other and the vision of a new and better life that we found the will to go on and create something beautiful for those who will follow us.

Through this experience, we learned much about the nature of reality and how it shifts with the attitude and imagination of the beings who perceive it. Where once there was much destruction and despair, new visions created beauty and the proliferation of new life and new ways of living. Once we realized that the reality of the world around us was the vibrational match to our own feelings and vision, we found new ways of thinking that created the new reality for ourselves. As we learned to play with this vision of reality, we found incredible new ways of governing and running our world that we had never had the courage to think of and implement before. It was only through being at the absolute lowest vibration that we were able to clearly see the profound changes that were created when we raised that vibration with a new-found motivation to make a better lives for ourselves.

Of course, we could have chosen differently, which would have created a much different future for ourselves, but as it was, we were convinced by the small triumphs to continue to work with the energy of our vision and try implementing new ways of commerce, agriculture, government and education. While none of these systems that we have implemented can be said to be perfect, they have, together, created surging growth, optimism and abundance within our communities where there was once only sadness and despair.

It is important that you understand the huge implications of this shift in perspective, as you are in the midst of your own perspective shift on your world.

We saw in our own experience how power and greed creates corrupt systems which then lead to a sort of mass brainwashing which is the only way to get the masses to go along with this corruption and accept it as the norm. This is what the political systems in your world are all about, and it is why many of these systems are being challenged. While there are many in power who are addicted to that sense of authority and righteousness, you also have some very strong leaders with a heart driven sense of compassion and empathy toward their constituents. It is important for you to know that not every politician is corrupt just by the nature of their posts and associations, but that the system as a whole is corrupted by the skewed sense of power that many have instilled upon their roles as leaders.

Therefore, it is important that these corrupt leaders be allowed to die out and be removed from their positions as newer, more forward-thinking leaders come into play. The media's derision of some power-hungry politicians is a sure sign that change is in the air, and that the old regime is about to fall. There will be those who will feel a sense of fear and despair about these shifts, as they have been led to believe that this is the signal of the apocalypse, but rest assured that the four horsemen will not be galloping into your towns anytime soon! The changes will ensure in a much gentler way, through new, kinder and more altruistic leaders who emerge in many areas of your government. This shift has already begun with your current president, although his power to instigate change is often limited by the restrictive systems placed on his position.

In the long run, those with the clearest vision for the future of the planet will win out, and those whose greed and desire for power will continue to be recognized as the source of many of the ills of your society and will shrink into the background. While these changes will not happen overnight, they will continue to accelerate as the people demand more and more the elimination of corrupt and damaging policies and leaders.

This does not in any way mean that any one party will become more dominant than the other; in fact, these changes will require the elimination of a party system altogether. Once again, this will be a difficult pill to swallow for many, and it will be met with much fear and ridicule from those who have only ever known the political system to operate in this way. However, it will soon become apparent, as it did for us, that without a party system, leaders can be voted in strictly on the merits of their experience and abilities, rather than their affiliations and financial success. This will create a whole new structure of government which will be fairer, more conscious and less self-serving. This is our vision for your world's future.

The changes that are currently occurring in your country's medical system are indicative of the elimination of class-based structures which allow only the wealthy access to specialized care and which create increased poverty and homelessness among those who are not in the upper echelons of society. As systems of health care become more standardized and accessible to all, it will become more and more apparent that this structure must be applied in all systems of services and goods which are necessary for a quality of life. This is what will eventually lead to the massive shifts in commerce and education, and eventually, the elimination of your current monetary system.

While you may imagine the breakdown of these systems as causing great chaos and confusion in your world, this is not necessarily the case. While there will be much confusion and backlash, when people begin to understand how the new systems work and the benefits of the shift, they will become more accepting and grateful for the changes. This, of course, will take time and patience, and it is clear to us that your world has plenty of both, although not everyone operates under this premise with the current structures.

Thus, it is important to understand that the nature of your reality is completely and totally based on your view of it. Your reality is a created one, which can be shifted and changed by your perception. There were many in our world who viewed the massive changes that occurred as the end times, and some even took their own lives in fear of what lay ahead. Others preferred to hole themselves up in shelters, believing that some great force was about to invade their lives and force them into some sort of altered state of reality through mind control and deception. These were similar to your government conspiracy theorists, who live under the delusion that all authority is out to get them and destroy their free will. Some of these people continue to live in their closed societies, refusing to conform to the new systems that have been developed. They are left to their own devices.

In all of these cases, these beings have created their own perception of reality from which they will not be swayed. As we became more in tune with this theory about the nature of reality and how it rests with the observer, we were able to be more compassionate with those who were skeptical about what we were trying to achieve, as we knew it was only through the observation of the success of these systems that some of these skeptics would shift their view of reality to one of promise and hope.

There is an increasing number of people in your societies who choose to live their lives in an optimistic way, doing all they can to find their own peaceful state of being through the love of others and through charitable works and acts of kindness. There are those who find great fulfillment through working with various causes and environmental and societal assistance program which seek to preserve and protect those people and natural habitats which are under threat through exploitation and corruption. There are still others who seek to expand the consciousness of others through spiritual work and counseling, and it is through their empathy and compassion that many are finding their own inner sense of peace and self-love which is harmonizing with the huge vibrational shifts currently occurring in your atmosphere.

These are the true leaders of your society right now. These are the visionaries who are following the call of their hearts to create a difference in the world they live in, and in the people who they understand are a part of themselves. This army of visionaries is growing exponentially, and they will be the ones who will lead your world into the new phase of its evolutionary growth.

Within the chaos of change there is a silent, still center of peace. There is a calm that can be found in knowing that change is occurring and that the things that need to be altered are being carried through the process of change. As you navigate your way through these days of seemingly unrelenting negative energy from those who see no hope or even a sense of purpose within the world, know that these feelings are temporary, and that they arise from the growing pains of a new society. You will be amazed at how your world will look in just a few short years. The acceleration of the energetic shift coupled with the outrage of those who are awake will continue to cause great shifts in the systems which need to change, and change they will.

Many turn to their ideas of God and religion as they travel paths of uncertainty, and there are some who fear the wrath and punishment of an omnipresent being who sees all and judges the deeds of His creations. We would like you to understand that the God of your holy books is not necessarily an accurate representation of what the Supreme Being really is.

First, there is no gender of this being, and there is no race, sexual orientation or physical characteristics of God. God is the Divine Intelligence out of which all beings and all matter were created. As such, God is not responsible for any of the roads you choose to travel, and any of the calamities that might befall you in this life. While there may be great comfort to be obtained through praying to God, and the people who attend church can find great commiseration and community, one does not need to pray or attend church to attract the attention of our most benevolent and loving Divine Being. There are always many unseen beings available to you at any time, and so your prayers will attract the highest powers to assist in whatever it is that is causing you distress.

The highest angelic beings that come to you will stand guard, initiate healing, help you draw necessary people and resources into your situation and simply provide comfort and peace with their presence near you.

Know that there are many hosts of angels around you at any given moment, and all you need to do is ask for their assistance with whatever it is you struggle with. You are surrounded at all times with various entities; angles, passed on loved ones, friends who have gone before and animal spirits. When you learn to tune in to their wisdom, you will find great guidance and loving counsel is to be gained from encounters with them.

Among those who work to secure an optimistic future for the planet and its inhabitants are those who conduct their lives in such a way as to rejoice in the gift that it is, and proceed through their lives in this way, with gratitude and forgiveness at every turn. These folks have within them the spark of light that is the gift of the Universe, and they are not afraid to let it shine. These are the people who will help to secure the future of the planet through their efforts at spreading kindness and peace throughout the world with small acts and deeds performed for no other reason than it is what they are called to do from their heart. These people are the messengers of the Divine and they have much to teach others about the true meaning of life and the real nature of reality. Many of these people have either limited or excessive religious training which may have limited their thinking at one time, but they all have the ability to respond to the call of their heart without question, believing it is their duty as a citizen of the planet to assist and care for their fellow beings, whether they be human or animal.

When one gives of their heart without the expectation of reward or recognition, they are reflecting the light of the Divine onto the world, thus assuring that this work will continue to be passed along from the warmth that is achieved in the hearts that are touched by that kindness. As we go about our daily lives, absorbed in busy-ness and obligation, it is essential that we find time to assert our right to display kindness and charity in whatever way we can. It is through these small acts that we truly achieve the ascension of our souls and feel the true meaning of happiness during this lifetime.

Many of these kind-hearted individuals respond with kindness because they themselves have known great unkindness, and they wish to treat others as they would have liked to be treated. This is a sacred choice and one that is not made lightly. When one is treated harshly as a child or has had great tragedy or cruelty in their lives, the choice to follow a life of kindness is a very difficult one, as the heart is often full of bitterness and rage, which, when left unexpressed, can preclude any heart-centered giving or truth-based kindness to occur to those around them. Understand when you least feel like giving is when you need to do it most, just as when you least feel like showing gratitude, that is the most important time for you to show it.

Those who give from their hearts with no expectation of reward know the great joy that can be found in such giving and as such, are rewarded tenfold every time they offer a good deed. In this way, a selfless act can be viewed as selfish, as there is a great reward to be felt in the heart of the giver. That is why they often will offer their assistance even when they are preoccupied with other matters or when they know there is no remuneration to be had from the deed. Understand that the smallest act of kindness, be it a kind word, a smile, a light touch of affection or simply an energetic presence can greatly alter the course of someone's life and, in fact, the world. The shift in energy that occurs at these times is far-reaching and quite powerful, and so it is quite important for you not to withhold your energy from kindness.

There are many kind people in your world, but they are largely the unsung heroes, the background players who never receive credit or acknowledgement for what they do. But as it has been stated, they feel their lives are greatly rewarded by the appreciation and love they feel every time they go out of their way to assist someone else.

This is not to say that the lower energies of selfishness, cruelty, hatred and wrath do not have their place, as they most certainly do. Although it is usually our desire to avoid or eliminate negative energy and hurtful experiences, it is important to realize the growth and awareness that can arise out of them. If we exercise our divine free will and freedom of choice when confronted with these challenges, the difference in the effect they can have on our lives is enormous. When faced with any challenge, it is important to take a wide perspective of it as soon as you can, since when we are embroiled in the thick of it, it is difficult to extract ourselves from it long enough to see it in the real context of our lives and the actual issue itself. When we dwell in the minutia of the issue, we often experience extreme frustration and helplessness which lead to stress and tension, which is unhealthy for the body, the mind and the soul. You are well aware of the dangers of prolonged stress on the body, but often we turn to escapism to deal with these issues rather than exercising our right to choose a different response to the things that cause us the most stress.

When faced with stressful situations, it is important to ask yourself some questions:

1. What can I do to alter the situation? Is there something I can put my energy into which will alter the energy of the situation, perhaps help someone to change their mind, move around some physical elements to shift the energy, or use compassion and forgiveness to dissolve resentment or obstinance? If there is some action that can be taken, do it and be done with it.

2. Is there a possibility that you can learn to alter your expectations so that the situation does not appear so incongruous to you? Perhaps a shift in your attitude could have far-reading effect on the situation and any relationships it affects.

3. If you are unable to alter the situation or your attitude about it, then it may be time to leave the situation altogether. Although this may seem like a big leap, it is sometimes better to leap into the unknown that to stay stuck in a known unhappiness, even when you are quite comfortable with the routine of that unhappiness.

There is always a choice to be made, and a lot can be learned in the process of making those choices. You may not believe yourself to be a strong or wise person but when faced with a true dilemma that is challenging your views about yourself, you may find that you possess more strength and wisdom than you ever thought you did, and you may find yourself able to deal with a difficult situation better than you ever imagined you could. This is the true test of your character and the real opportunity to develop a clearer identity and stronger self-confidence, should you so choose.

This leads us to a discussion about the choices you make concerning what to believe about your life, your world and the Universe in general. There are many who believe only in cold, hard facts; however, there is much that is not known about the universe and about your origins as human beings, and there are those who believe that all beings were created by the hand of God as full and complete, as in the Adam and Eve stories in your Bible. It is important that you understand that there is no religion to muddy the waters of your belief systems unless you let it in.

As for the origins of life, know that there is no one absolute truth. There is much to be said for scientific theories and there has been fascinating work done by scientists which pinpoint dates and cataclysms in the universe which sparked the origins of life; however, science alone cannot answer all the questions about the absolute origins of life and where the soul departs to at the end of life. There are huge gaps of understanding in your scientific analysis of life; however, there is also great knowledge that has arisen through scientific inquiry. No one system of belief or thinking has all the answers, and that is why it is important for science and metaphysics to come together to dissolve some of the myths and misconceptions about your earthly beginnings.

The limitations placed on the beliefs of the masses through religious control has caused much consternation from those of us who now know and understand that the truths are so much broader than anything any religion can fathom. There are many truths which religion avoids, and it's important that we look to science for some of these truths, but it's also important to realize that science can create doubts in people's ability to discern truths through their own inner senses, and not just through concrete, proven facts. As humans, you are always more comfortable with that which can be proven and shown to be true through irrefutable evidence; however, there are truths which will never be shown in this way, and limiting our ability to obtain the truth to these irrefutable methods eliminates much information which is discerned only through the higher senses. Your scientific advances are nearing the point of factual saturation, which means the only place left to explore will be the higher realms which are outside of that which can be proven in a scientific or intellectual way. These are the areas into which quantum mechanics delves, and while there is much resistance to the integration of science and spirit, it is becoming more prevalent for the highest scientific minds to admit that there is much to be learned in the metaphysical aspects of existence and reality.

Your scientists are beginning to acknowledge the existence of matter that has been previously unknown, and universal anomalies which were heretofore thought of as impossible. It is necessary for these exciting discoveries to be made, and they will continue to create more and more questions for the scientific community to explore about the nature of what is called reality and its place in the time and space continuum. The discovery of the "God Particle," for instance, has created far more questions than its proven existence has answered, as have the discoveries in the universe of warped space and condensed energy unlike anything that has ever been seen before. There are many experiments going on now which are not shared openly with the public, and they involve breaking the barriers of space travel and extending life beyond anything that has ever been dreamed of before. Some of these experiments will be wildly successful, and some will fail, but all of them will open up new avenues of exploration which will always lead to a questioning of consciousness , energy and the realm of spiritual awareness.

The darkest reaches of space have always been thought to contain great expanses of nothingness; however, this is proving to be an untruth. These areas of space are actually teeming with energy and various forms of consciousness which are difficult for the human mind to grasp, although the existence of these things has long been known to your most prominent physicists. There are magnetic shifts occurring in these far depths of space which are allowing them to be seen in quick glimpses on the instruments of some astrophysicists, and there is quite a lot of conjecture going on over this new information which has not been made public in any way. There are those who believe it is simply a malfunction of their equipment, but others are feeling intuitively that they are on the brink of discovering something truly outstanding. It will be quite a long while before any type of conclusion is made which will satisfy the majority of those involved, and until then, these discoveries and experiments will be largely hidden from the public.

Within the realm of scientific discovery lies a host of hidden truths which are controlled largely by those who wish to keep the public under false pretenses of lack and limitation. This is not in any way related to those who are deeply engrossed in conspiracy theories, although it is true that the greed and monopoly of the large corporations who sponsor these scientific activities can dictate that which is divulged to the public and that which is either brushed aside as faulty or simply hidden. As the power of the megalithic corporate entities dissolves, these truths will begin to become known, and you will find that many of the things you have thought are undiscovered or unknown have actually been proven and developed for quite a long time. These things include certain cures for diseases, energy-reducing mechanisms and space travel and exploration. It is important that you maintain a wise and prudent skepticism when it comes to what you are led to believe by the media and the scientific and medical journals, as these entities are not independent of the corporations who sponsor and control them.

Herein lies the truth: those who are in the midst of raising their vibratory awareness through a calling which is leading them to explore their consciousness and through the energetic shifts of your planet and the Universe are beginning to get glimpses of the truth which has been hidden from the general public for so long. As this information becomes more and more mainstream, there will be those who demand disclosure and in the end, they will win it. But there is no need to wait until information is made public; you all have the abilities to tune into higher truths through your intuition and higher consciousness which can be reached through states of meditation and quiet inner study. All beings have access to this state, but very few deign to examine it.

It is our hope that through the publication of this book, our words will inspire many of those who read it to do some inner exploration to discern their own truths. This inner spiritual study will help raise the consciousness of your civilization as people discover that they have been accepting truths which have been forced upon them by those who wish to profit and gain from those misguided ideas. For now, it is simply important that you are aware that not all of the information you receive is the absolute truth, and in fact, even those things that have truthful elements to them are filtered and orchestrated to create a view of reality which is in accordance with a need to consume, a need to live in a fear of lack, and the need to fear death. When one goes within to find his or her own truth, it will be found that none of these fears actually exists except outside of oneself.

This is where the true benefit of the exploration of the inner self lies; discovering that which is divine and immortal within oneself removes us from the fear and dependency of those institutions outside of us which we have become so reliant upon. The resultant empowerment and freedom will allow your civilization to advance in far greater ways than has heretofore been allowed, and these advances will be what saves your civilization from extinction and ruination through greed and ambivalence and disregard for the sanctity of all life. The truth cannot be found in the sanctimony of the church, nor in the sterility of the laboratory or the hypocrisy of the boardroom, but only within the recesses of our own minds, our own hearts and in the light of the spirit. This is where true limitless space exists, within oneself, and the more this is acknowledged as a legitimate and crucial field of study and exploration, the faster advances can be allowed to occur in the quality of life on your planet.

Of course, there will be those who feverishly resist these studies as being anything other than frivolous mind games which serve no purpose other than to confuse and mislead the public. But there are already many in existence who are now heeding the call to a higher consciousness, and who are receiving higher information as is being given through the words of this book. It is through the efforts of these extraordinary individuals that the greatest advances will be made, and that the naysayers will be proven incorrect in their assumptions about scientific truths and spiritual hogwash. It will continue to become increasingly clear that only through the integration of science and spirit will the real solutions to the biggest challenges of your planet be resolved.

Chapter Three ~ Where the Trail Ends

In this chapter, we would like to examine the issue of physical death. It is a subject that we feel deserves quite a bit of careful consideration, as your culture's ideas about it have been so heavily influenced and have become filled with fear and despair.

We would like you to consider that death of the physical body does not constitute the death of the spiritual aspect of being, or the soul. This essence of our being is who we really are, and it is not subject to the laws of life and death, of decay and regeneration, as it is purely energetic and therefore perpetual. The energy essence of the body, or the soul, survives in its natural state outside of the physical body, and therefore, death of the physical is allowing that spiritual aspect to return to its natural state of being. The return of spirit to the non-physical state creates a joyful feeling of release from the bonds of the physical life, and the spirit rejoices with its freedom and departure from whatever illness, pain or suffering it may have been experiencing in the material world.

The passage of our souls into the non-physical reality of the other side involves several stages. Upon leaving the body, the spirit is greeted by any loved ones in spirit who have taken on the role of guard or guide to the other side. The deceased may see former loves, family members and pets as they cross, and in fact, they may often see these spirits before they cross over.

As one begins her transition to the other side, those around her may think she is hallucinating when she experiences contact with the lost loved ones who have come to help with the transition. Know that these visions are quite real, and that they can bring great comfort and joy to the soul of the person who is in the midst of her transition. The souls who appear to assist with the transition are chosen very carefully, as they help to guide the essence of the departing soul into its new state of being.

Although we are quite different physically from you, our soul is the same and thus, our transition into the next world is very much the same as well. We have done much research into the death phenomenon and have ourselves conversed with the souls of departed beings from our world to find out what the transition is like, and we find that the most prevalent feeling at the time of departure is great peace and love. There is no fear and no pain involved in their passage, only a sense of wonder and joyful release from the heavy burdens of physical life.

Since your scientific studies have been unable to prove anything about the afterlife, spirit or the death experience in terms of the etheric body, much conjecture has been made about it being merely a physical reaction to the body's demise and the shutdown of the brain. Any other theory about the transition of the soul is often met with much derision and skepticism because of the lack of material evidence; however, if the scientific community could simply allow itself to stretch the limits of absolute proof and delve more deeply into the study of the metaphysical aspects of life as being just as real and vital as the physical aspects, much of the fears and horror around death would begin to dissipate, creating a much healthier acceptance of this life passage.

We mourn our dead much as you do, but we do not see death as the end of life; thus, we are able to accept the aspect of death as being that of a transition, rather than an ending, which helps us to face death and deal with it in a much healthier way. We know that it is only a matter of time before we are reunited with our loved ones, and we also know that we are able to communicate with them even if we are not able to hear and see them in the traditional sense. Our rituals around death are more like celebrations, where we honor the deceased by ushering them into their new lives with music, song and happy memories. We know that the tears we shed are temporary, and that the soul of our loved one is now free to experience itself on a much higher level than it was able to do while in a material existence. Thus, we rejoice in the transition and perform little rituals which are thought to ease the transition and welcome the soul back home.

As we have found the means to release our spiritual essence from our living beings without much disruption to our physical lives, we find that we can also converse with the spirits of those who have passed on while we are in this state. We are able to experience their state of being, albeit temporarily, and we can tell you that it is a beautiful and natural state of being which is impossible to experience in a material aspect of life. Without the burdens of body, responsibility, pain, anguish and self-defeating beliefs, the soul is free to experience itself in its purest form, and it's able to connect with loved ones both living and in spirit on the highest level. There is no limit to what the soul can experience in this state, and all of the issues that plagued the person in life melt away to nothingness. Only in this state can the true essence of your being experience the true meaning of life and the absolute connection of all life on the highest soul level.

There is much to be gained in the study and exploration of death with the intention of changing long-established fears and beliefs surrounding it. Much of our suffering in life comes from the fear of death and the loss of loved ones. As we begin to accept the cycle of life and our inevitable demise, these fears soften and we are more apt to find reasons to enjoy the life we have been blessed with as the true miracle that it is.

Understand that your soul often leaves the body when your conscious mind is asleep, and that the events of your dreams sometimes reflect the journey your soul is taking while in this altered state of reality. While not every dream is reflective of this soul travel, you may found that certain dreams stand out as most vivid or hyper real. These dreams may provide you with much-needed insight about your life's journey, and so it's important to keep track of them. However, know that every dream has its own effect on your higher self and your subconscious mind. It is often a very useful exercise to keep track of your dreams and look to them for higher guidance and wisdom which may come in the form of puzzles and metaphors that only you can figure out.

The complex nature of the soul allows it to experience multiple states of being and to express itself in ways that we in the material world of the conscious mind could never fully understand. Without the need for the construct of time, the soul is able to experience past, present and future as its present state of reality, should it so choose. It is able to recall incidents from past lives, and relive them quite vividly, if this is deemed necessary to understand the learning that was prompted by various incidents. When the soul is free from the limitations of the mind, it is able to wander at will, and can experience states of being which transcend any that you could ever imagine. The beauty of the life of the soul cannot be matched, even in the most glorious aspects of your material world.

It is this pure essence of who you are that has deemed it appropriate for you to incarnate at this particular time, with this particular life, with the personality and character traits that you possess, and the family and geographical location that you're now in. It is through the efforts of your soul that you are able to experience the multi-faceted journey of a life span, complete with its challenges and joys, losses and heart connections, learning and growing. Every day you are faced with the choices which build the structure of your life's path, and which afford you the opportunity to create the most lucrative path for your soul's wisdom and experience. This life may not always seem so important to you, but it is the most sacred of blessings.

As death is the ultimate fate of all living things, it is vitally important that we deal with it in a more open and healthy way, so that the finality of that ending does not cause us to feel hopeless and unimportant. Your soul will go through multiple transitions from life and death, through various dimensional shifts, through many levels of consciousness on the other side (which are too complex to explain) and through the physical changes of aging, health issues and family challenges. These challenges can be viewed as painful beyond measure and unfair, or they can be viewed as higher learning experiences from which we can rise above and move forward.

Your human existence is the ultimate creation of your own levels of consciousness, and much of what your experience, including your emotions, your pains, your suffering, is all a product of your intellectual consciousness, which believes it can organize the world in such a way that it makes sense and where everything within this framework of a life can be neatly categorized and labeled to make it easier to understand. This often sets you up for great debates in the classroom, in the political arena and in the family home about the nature of reality and the true essence of who we are vs. who we let the world see. You may even debate with yourself about what your real truth really is, and whether it resides in the tangible aspects of the material world which are perceived through the five senses, or if the real truth is something unseen with the eyes but felt with the heart and sensed with the soul. We say it is a combination of both, and that the deeper soul experience can often provide us with the strength of character needed to survive some of the most difficult life challenges.

We find that as we allowed the expression of some of the deepest primal urges of our souls, which include the need for ritual, the need for a deep connection with our natural surroundings, a need to give and receive love, a need to protect and serve those we love and the place we call home, and the need to procreate and experience intimacy, the more we feel connected to our highest essence as well as our deep roots of physical existence. There was a time in our history where we suppressed many of these base primal needs in the name of technological evolution, but we found the disconnection that ensued caused us to evolve to the brink of destruction. Honoring our deepest soul urges helped put us back on track with our true purpose and our happiest state of oneness and community with all living beings. We have observed that many of your people who are experiencing an awakening of the soul are being drawn to return to these primal connections which incite compassion and deep love for all of existence. These emotional instincts are what will spur the movement to create a more harmonious existence for all of your planet's inhabitants.

Within the soul are many layers of consciousness which relate to the various levels of awareness. Your scientific study has only uncovered a few of these layers of consciousness, but there are really many more. The mind can access only a small part of the soul through the conscious and subconscious mind; it is only when those levels are not active that the other levels can become realized. This is usually through sleep, or through the use of psychotropic substances which alter the state of consciousness to the degree that the deeper levels can be realized.

Of course, these many levels are always active within the soul and they process much information that is vital to the ascension and progression of the soul's journey. It is an untrue assumption that only the information brought into your awareness by the conscious mind is pertinent to your life's experience. Actually, there is much more going on which the conscious mind is not aware of, but which is coming into play in the development of your sense of reality. For instance, when this channel, Tracy, is accessing the spirit world or communicating with us, there is a very different part of consciousness being activated which does not involve the usual modes of thinking and reasoning. If she were to be tested during these times, it would be discovered that the process does not involve her intellect much at all, except for that which is needed to record the information that is being processed. This is why much of what she receives is not stored in her memory. It is not processed through the normal modes of thought and perception which would normally be passed on to the memory part of the brain, and as such, it is easily forgotten.

As you begin to realize that you are not limited by your five senses in your experiences of the world, reality and the universe, you will begin to accept the fact that your other, higher senses play just as important a role in the nature of what your experience. While the five senses are miraculous in themselves, there is much mystery and truth that can come from the higher senses such as psychic awareness, intuition, emotional awareness and energetic connection. For those who are able to integrate all of these aspects of human awareness, their life experience is made so much richer and fuller, and they are able to access levels of peace and trust not available to those who only count on their senses of sight, sound, touch, taste and smell to determine their own sense of reality.

The body has an emotional brain which is just as powerful, if not more so, than the cranial brain. It is the heart, and its function is not limited to being the body's blood pump. It is the seat of compassion, love and understanding, and as such, it transmits and receives powerful energetic impulses regarding the emotional well-being of its host and others. There is much to be said of one who is in touch with his own heart and follows its advice in all matters of his world.

As the heart opens to give and receive love, it also causes powerful electrical impulses which can cause great healing to occur in the organisms around it. This love is one of the greatest healing powers in the universe, and its energy can be harnessed to affect great physical, emotional and mental healing in those who are experiencing the power of love. The spiritual healing that takes place when in the presence of unconditional love cannot be duplicated, and it is the goal of many to experience this in one form or another.

The absence or withdrawal of love can cause anomalous behavior which is a call for help, affection and caring. Most beings who have felt the absence of love and caring will resort to unusual measures to completely fill the void that is left when love is not present. It is important that we see certain behaviors as a cry for love, and not necessarily evil. This will help the assessment of treatment for those whose emotional lives have become unbalanced to such a degree that their ideas of right and wrong become blurred, and they no longer feel the moral conscious necessary to avoid damaging behavior.

Of course, the healthiest form of love is self-love; however, this form of love has been largely discouraged in your culture as it is empowering and freeing, and in many sectors of your society, these are not seen as valuable assets. Therefore, the idea of self-love has been sermonized as selfishness and conceit. Religions speak of self-love as the work of the devil, and preach that all is to be done in service to a higher power. In all cultures, the will of the child is bent and skewed into servitude of the parent, the teacher, the employer, the government, and all other forms of authority, leaving little room for self-care and self-love. It is vital to your civilization that humankind returns to a healthier outlook on what it means to care for the self without ego or self-aggrandizement. As the energy shifts around your planet, and consciousness begins to rise, those without a clear sense of themselves and their value to the world will feel left behind. They will not feel a clear sense of purpose as your culture begins its new awakening to a more spiritual consciousness which values all life and considers kindness more important than profit or gain. Those who have no sense of this will not know what to do with themselves, as they have completely tied their sense of identity with the need for wealth and power. As the value of those things diminishes, so will the will of those who have no other sense of purpose in the world. This is why it's so important that people begin to recognize the need for self-love. It is through that awakening of the divine nature of all beings that people will begin to feel their true calling in the world and will find that their previous attachments are no longer necessary.

In more primitive times, your civilization recognized the divine nature of all life. There were many rituals which marked the changing seasons and the connection between the material world and the divine. Ancient man felt himself as an expression of this higher power and understood that that power lived within himself, as well as outside on the ethereal plane. Through celebration, ritual and clear knowledge of oneself, these people felt they best appeased the gods and thus assured the rich blessings of the universe would be poured upon them.

It is time for your civilization to return to those ancient roots of ritual celebration, compassionate self-care, communion with spirit and a higher power and increased community involvement. Through all of these ventures, mankind is placed within a bond of divine love and the highest spiritual light which raises the vibration and increases sensitivity to unseen forces. This sensitivity, coupled with an increased awareness of the unity of all things, will be what moves your world's civilizations into the new age.

Chapter Four ~ The Scientific Mindset

Your civilization has learned to worship science almost as much as it worships its own idea of God, the Father and the Universe. The scientific mind is seen as the forerunner of all other schools of thought. It is seen as the noblest of endeavors to seek proof of various theories; however, you should know that very little has ever been proven beyond a shadow of a doubt, and that even the most rudimentary theories are still being tested and found to have caveats.

In space exploration, for instance, scientists are finding that many of the things they once concluded as irrefutable proof in previous days are now being called into question as their instruments find ways to track the evolution of the Universe and its many galaxies and planets.

Previously it was felt that scientific theory, when practiced accurately, could lead to no mistakes with calculations, or deviations caused by energetic forces, or simply the playfulness of spirit. Science, therefore, is in itself a form of religious belief based on what is thought to be irrefutable evidence gathered from repeated experimentation. Scientists will see themselves as the ultimate authority in determining the nature of realty and the universe, and they will mostly scoff at any other theory that is not based on scientific theory and dutifully prepared experiment.

We would like you to know that all experiments are flawed, and that most of the time, the conclusions that are reached are false, as they have been performed under outmoded and outdated theories of time and space.

When the outcomes of these experiments are projected into the future, one can see how they are flawed in the way they gather data and run prescribed tests on matter in such a way that the actual experiment is manipulating and affecting the way the matter itself behaves. Since the idea that human energy can affect the outcome of experiments with matter is not taken into account and repeated results which indicate a certain outcome are taken as the truth of the theory, in fact, it is a skewed result.

Scientists are finding that some experimental procedures are causing some disagreement within their ranks as to the actual theory their results are proving. Sometimes, the results do not seem to match the theory they are testing, since the matter behaved in such an unexpected way. However, when this happens, the data will be discarded in favor of another measurement which achieves the familiar result. Without taking into account the results that have been discarded, how can any statistical framework be developed which provides accurate data and allows for deviations which can show the conscious manipulation of matter simply by observing it?

Scientific experimentation and theory have made great strides in your civilization; however, it has come to a standstill in many fields of study, not because of a lack of funding or brainpower, but because the results of some experiments are discounted as flawed, when in fact they are producing some amazing results. The corporate funding institutions have a lot to say about what is released to the public and where their money is spent, so it is important that you realize that what you are shown and what is released are not always the complete truth.

There are many cures for pervasive diseases which have not been shared with the public for various reasons. This, however, will change greatly once your monetary system shifts. When monetary gain is no longer an issue and large corporate entities can no longer control the release of data, you will find how much has been hidden from you for many decades.

With the release of the money factor and the decriminalization of certain substances, allowing them to be experimented with in a broader way, many tried and tested results will be able to be released to the general public and they will find that many of the things currently shared by what appear to be fringe elements are in fact true, and that simple cures are available which had never been thought of before, since their findings from these experiments were discarded as false.

For instance, there are cures available right now for hereditary lung disorders such as cystic fibrosis which can alter the lifestyles of those who suffer from it, as well as prolong their lives. There are very powerful treatments of cancer available which avoid the sometimes lethal side effects of chemotherapy. There are natural cures affected with herbal and homeopathic remedies which have been avoided by the medical community as being too primitive or out of the realm of the scientific inquiry. These are actually very powerful medicines, especially when combined with spiritual purging.

As scientific advances continue, researchers will continue to find that they are forced to consider some spiritual aspects of their studies which they would rather avoid. However, the overlap of spirituality and science is a necessary component of some of the more advanced scientific theories.

When one studies the nature of the universe, matter and life, and those studies go as far as they can to an atomic level, there are limited subsequent options for study which do not include various theories on the nature of reality outside of the usual scientific path. There is still much to be learned about the material aspects of matter and the universe, but the true origins of this matter is a realm of inquiry which must at some point be considered other than by relegating all to chance.

As consciousness evolves, so will the human brain, and the division between the left and right brain will continue to blur, leaving little room for the separation of logical ideas from spiritual ones. There is a true nature of all that exists which transcends the ideas of pure matter and chance, and which infers a higher consciousness which is just as real and measurable as any material or energetic subject. Once your scientists begin to understand how to harness and work with the power of the mind and soul, great advances will be made in the fields of space travel, environmental reclamation and creating a non-monetary structure.

There will soon be a scientific revolution of sorts, which breaks the barrier of spiritual or metaphysical studies and embraces many of those studies which current scientists regularly scoff at. These studies will create amazing progress in not only the study of mankind, but its very salvation.

Your species will eventually leave the planet in search of a more stable environment, and by that time, the idea of space travel will be quite mainstream and many far reaches of the universe will have been explored in one way or another. Humankind will live on, far beyond the life of your sun and any other nearby planetary systems.

Your scientific community has achieved amazing things in a very short period of time, and it is very true that your civilization has begun to advance at a far more rapid pace than ever before. There have been huge advancements made in your methods of communication and digital technology which has enabled vast amounts of information to be shared and studied by huge numbers of people all over your world. This is just the beginning, though, and it is important that you recognize the infinite benefits of this technology as it can be used to create a new world order which is based on a unity of thought, ideas and culture. By joining massive numbers of people through technology, you have created a world which is more unified and less separate in its quest for peaceful coexistence and compassion. This will be the leading edge of the changes which will spark global shifts in the way your world is run.

It is vital that the leaders of this consciousness revolution see beyond the short-sighted aims of those who simply see these technological advances as commodities and commercial boons to be exploited and marketed to the masses. These advances are the forerunners of a new wave of global communication which links less developed countries with those who can help them and countries with ecological emergencies with those who need to become more aware of the areas where your world is in need of attention.

Education, awareness, economic assistance and personal connection will all help to heal the ills of many in your world if these become the aims of those who have access to the quickly evolving technology that is so readily available to all. When one observes the technology available today in comparison with what was available just a mere 50 years ago, the miracle of this advancement can truly be felt. The question now is how these advances will be utilized to assist in the evolution of your world, rather than in its social decomposition.

It is solely in the hands of those who have access to these electronic devices how they choose to view them. There are those who choose to see them as a threat to the current world order, creating a culture of digitally-addicted people who no longer have the personal social interaction of their forebearers, or it can be viewed as a method to bring the world closer together and unite its population in the spirit of healing, cleaner living and compassionate giving. This has always been the choice when any advancements are made in the field of science and technology, and there will always be those who resist change and who see any move toward a more advanced culture as a move away from the traditions and rituals which make them feel grounded and safe. But the fact remains that these two aspects of life can exist harmoniously and that technology can be utilized in such a way that the old core values can be not only preserved, but enhanced.

A scientific community which embraces, rather than shuns, spiritual energy as a very real aspect of life, will create advances far beyond that which have already be made, and will begin to unfold the mysteries about the nature of reality which will lead to a more peaceful, compassionate and gentle way of life which resonates with the energy of each individual's soul. This will be when science will truly reach the far reaches of the Universe.

Chapter Five ~ Tumbling Through Time

There is a belief that time is linear, since that is the way it is experienced, with a clear sense of past, present and future. It is a deliberate creation of the human mind to arrange its perception of life in this manner; any other way would be chaotic and difficult to assimilate with the limitations of the brain. Separating our lives into a linear order allows us to experience progression and order.

In the broader view of the Universe, time does not exist quite like that. It is a difficult concept to grasp, but all of time actually exists at once. In fact, there are many times in our lives when we have an instant of crossing the timelines and entering a past or future existence. These are only a fraction of a second in time, but they happen quite frequently as we proceed through the rather fragile construct of linear time.

For example, if you were to take an orange and decide to eat it, you know that in the linear mode of time you would have steps to perform before you could get to the juicy heart of the matter. First you would have to pick up the orange, score it and begin to peel the skin. Then you would section or cut it into smaller bits which are easier to chew, and then you would begin to eat it. Each task is thusly broken down into manageable steps which we know we have to accomplish before we can recognize our goal.

However, this time construct often causes us much pain and frustration, as it is something over which we feel we have no control, and which we often feel robbed of. In fact, your mind has much to do with the speed of time.

It is said that "Time flies when you're having fun," and this comes closer to the truth about time than most scientific theories. Our experience of time is directly related to our frame of mind and the occupation we find ourselves in at any given moment. Should you find yourself in a desperate situation, having lost everything and feeling hopeless and alone, you would probably experience a drag on time, where every moment seems to be forever and time would feel endless and torturous. In contrast, time spent on pleasurable pursuits seems to rush by at a much faster pace.

Time is actually a malleable construct. It is not as fixed as you might think, and your perception of it is not simply in your mind, per se. However, your mind does control the way you perceive time and you may notice some phenomena which support this belief such as the speeding up of time as you age and the slowing down of time when you are feeling in a negative or in a low-vibrational space. Your emotions and state of mind can have a lot to do with the way you are able to perceive time and the actual speeding up or slowing down of your own personal time experience.

As we have mentioned, there are multiple aspects to your soul and your life experiences, and some of these aspects exist in different times. Some of these times appear to you to be in the past, where you have lived and died in a different era. Actually, these past lives closely coincide with our own, even though you feel they happened quite a long time ago.

As we travel through the far reaches of the Universe to converse with you, it is as though time has been warped and shrunken so that we can have a shorter journey than would be expected in traveling such a long distance.

As we travel through space and time, we have found a way to surpass the limitations that are placed upon the perceptual aspects of linear time and space in terms of distance. As mentioned previously, we have discovered a way to project our soul bodies through wormholes in space which are areas where the time-space continuum does not adhere to the usual laws of physics. There is a cosmic warp present within these tunnels which allow travel over great distances in very brief moments of time. These wormholes exist in the areas of space where the universe experiences a shift in its energetic mass, thereby creating a dimensional porthole which bridges the higher dimensions through vast areas of space. While we were aware of these time portholes and had studied them for many decades, we were never able to discover how we would utilize them for space travel as we were quite sure that the extreme nature of the dimensional shift would not support life. It wasn't until we discovered the means to separate the conscious aspect of the multi-dimensional soul from the physical, self-conscious nature of life that we were able to discern the way these time-space warps could be utilized.

Your perception of time is also governed by the patterns which are delineated by the rotation of your planet and the day and night ratios it creates. The circadian rhythms create habits and rituals which delineate time and help you create a sense of order and balance. The way that your brain perceives time throughout your daily routine is not always the truth, however. There are constant shifts in time and a constant dimensional pulse which is not perceived by the brain, since it would confuse the order needed to maintain a sense of equilibrium and balance.

A good way to think of it is as if it were a filmstrip. You know that the film is actually made up of a series of still photographs which are fed through the projector in a stream which creates the perception of movement through time. Your brain is not perceiving the images as singular and pulsing, even though that is actually what is happening. It is similar to the perception of time and your sense of reality in that your vibrational pulsing through space and time is not actually a steady stream, but a constant shifting of energy through multi-dimensional space. Your human brain is only equipped to discern the steady stream of time, space and existence. But there is much more to it than that.

Your limited perception is not a curse, however, as it is what allows you to experience the progression of life and time which will best utilize your free will and ability to make choices and experience the many facets of your human existence as a progressive whole. Having a starting point, a middle and an end point in all of your life's paths allows you to see the progression of learning and advancement that is being offered to you through the experience of your incarnation.

With the question of the accuracy of the perception of time, comes the question of the feasibility of time travel. We want you to know that time travel is indeed possible and that you are doing it all the time without your knowledge. Part of the intermittent pulsing of your vibrational energy is a sort of travel through the many existences of your soul in various dimensions and times. As advances are made in the field of time/space continuum and the ability of the soul to transcend the known laws of physics and cross the boundaries of space and time, scientists will discover the means to manipulate the structure of time and therefore deliberately travel through the timeline to the past and the future.

There is some question among you about the sightings of craft and beings that you call UFOs and aliens, and there are those who believe that they are time travelers. We would like you to know that there have been some cases of your people encountering beings from the future traveling back through time to your reality, and there are also other beings from galaxies such as our own who continue to visit your world as a means of research the discovery. With the vast number of civilizations in the universe, there are bound to be some who discover the means of traveling great distances as we have, and use this ability to advance their knowledge of the universe and its inhabitants. There are those who seek other worlds as possible homes for their people, although none have generally populated your world at this time. The visitors often find that your world is inhospitable to their needs and seek elsewhere.

While there is much you do not know about your government's involvement with UFO research and discovery, there is nothing that would greatly alter your view of the world, and so there is little to be gained by it. Even with the divulgence of this information, there will be those who will find a way to maintain their disbelief, and others who will use fear to create a state of panic and worry that your world is being invaded by a hostile civilization, which has never been the case. There are those beings who are less cognizant of the effect on human beings of forced abduction and experimentation, although their intention is not to harm in any way. As they are limited in their emotional scope, so they are incapable of understanding the vast array of human emotions. They truly mean no harm .

Understand that the fear inherent in the belief and exploration of the existence of life outside of your planet will limit its scope and the success of any endeavor to prove such existence will always be met with harsh criticism, no matter what is found or proven. The capability to manipulate findings and cover up information which is deemed to be too explosive for the comfort and safety of your civilization has left a web of deceit and false stories being released. These stories only add to the confusion and the explanation of unexplained or unidentified phenomena which only leaves a mystery rather than a fact. This allows greater room for error and misrepresentation, and unfortunately creates a sense that those who have these experiences are unbalanced or liars, which in turn limits the propensity for those who have experiences to discuss and report them. There is much manipulation of data and undisclosed information which it is feared would create a less stable society. But it is also true that some of this knowledge would interfere with some of the work that is being done in the advancement of your civilization in that fear would distort that work and cause a distortion of its value.

While there are, in fact, many false stories told by those who are unstable or who seek attention, there are also many quite sane and intelligent humans who have had "unexplained" experiences which are very real and well documented. While it is advisable to read any such stories with the eye of a skeptic, it is also important that you trust your own inner knowing to tell you when these stories appear to be honest and true. Fear can cause huge distortions in the perception of reality, and it is for that reason that fear is often used as a method of control. Remember this, and know that fear is a choice, and that not everything that is unknown needs to be feared.

There are many thousands of worlds unknown to you, and you are known to some of them, due to their ability to cross the limitations of time and space and explore the vast reaches of the universe. Some will visit, and many others will not, but know that you are at all times safe and protected, even when these visits appear to be threatening and frightening. There is no danger of alien life forms invading your world with the intent to do any harm to you or your planet at this time. All space and time travel is done for the betterment of their own civilization through research and exploration.

There are many detailed records of encounters with unexplained crafts and beings, and the subsequent findings of the scientific experimentation which occurred in response to these reports. The records are quite hidden, and even those that are released contain misleading information so as to limit the trail of information which led to the research in the first place. There are those who know bits and pieces of this information, but very few who know it all, which is quite deliberate. Again, this is all being done with the intention of keeping the public feeling safe and secure, and avoiding the chaos that could result from widespread fear. In fact, there really is nothing at all to fear from any of these encounters. But it is important that you know they exist.

There are many other beings such as us who have discovered the means to travel through space and time to visit other worlds, and some do so with the intention of helping to guide, as we do, and others do so with the intention to learn and explore. We have never encountered any whose intentions were harmful or negative, as those civilizations who are advanced enough to discover the means of transcending the typical rules of time and space have progressed far beyond the need for violence and disregard for life. When a civilization advances to that degree, it is inevitable that its collective soul also advances, and this will not allow for the mentality of one who wishes to deliberately harm another living being.

Understand that you have vast beauty and an amazing array of life on your planet that is not typical of other worlds in the universe. While life exists in many forms, your planet is one of the richest in the form of diversity of life forms and even among the array of human beings. It is quite fascinating to the travelers of the universe, and so when they are able to perceive and study your planet, they will often do so with great interest. Only when your civilization is ready to accept otherworldly beings into its midst with kindness and compassion will they allow themselves to be openly perceived. While your civilization has made great strides in a very short period of time with its ability to accept the vast diversity just among your fellow human beings, there is still a long way to go before any other worldly beings will be willing to allow themselves to be perceived in a concrete way, lest they be obliterated out of fear and a lack of empathy and understanding.

Chapter Six ~ The Domino Effect

There is a paradigm within your culture which states that every action has an equal and opposite reaction, and this is mainly true in all areas of your physical world, but it is not necessarily applied to matters of the heart and soul. Once again, we want to stress that while the studies of science have contributed greatly to the progression of your culture and has advanced many avenues of medicine, exploration and understanding of the laws of the natural world, it fails to take into account the importance and reality of spirit. Because of this, we often try to apply the laws of nature as defined by scientific study to those things which have a more emotional base, and we wonder why we often feel that we have failed.

This is a major cause of struggle and suffering in your world. The laws which make understanding the world around you are clear and consistent, and so we expect those same laws to be as clear and consistent when it comes to the nature of the personality and the soul, but this is simply not the case. We cannot apply scientific theory to anything which is outside of the realms of scientific study, and the matters of the soul and heart do not follow the same patterns dictated by behavioral specialists. Human nature simply cannot be ascribed a certain formulaic pattern of living, feeling and experiencing life. The personal vibration and life path of each individual is such that they cannot possibly view their world in the same way as anyone else. Thus, we cannot ever say for certain that someone's behavior or emotional make-up will be predictable in every nuance.

This is not to say that certain patterns do not exist, and that those who study human behavior are wrong. But it is not correct to assume that simply because one is aware of certain patterns of thinking, or certain synapses of the brain which may be automatically programmed for certain types of behavior, that that in and of itself is the sole component which creates personality. For we are much more than the patterns of our brains.

It is important to understand that much thought and behavior does not originate in the brain, and that we do not create through the thought patterns which arise from the physical matter of that brain, but that thought and creation is the product of processing the vibrations of the soul. In other words, it is the programming of the soul which actually creates thought, and the brain is simply the processor. Thought comes from the intentions that you set within the ethereal energy of the soul. These thoughts are the result of the brain interpreting and responding to those vibrations. At the moment a feeling, idea or desire is fed into the brain from the higher vibration of the soul, the brain then processes through this data based on what it already knows. Thus, it decides to reject some of the data because it has been programmed to believe that it is unnecessary information, or that the desire is an impossible one. Therefore, it is the belief system formed from the interpretation of experience and the emotional history of the individual which actually forms the thoughts, but the initial trigger for the thought comes from the energy field outside of the physical body.

This is not something which your scientific community is ready to grasp or accept, as it is not provable or measurable just yet. But once this fact is discovered in a tangible way, the repercussions will be great. Not only will this be seen to prove the existence of the ethereal soul, it will also shatter old myths about death and the afterlife. The acceptance of this one truth about the nature of reality and the mind-body-soul connection will completely revolutionize the scientific community.

For if thoughts are not generated by the brain itself, it means that there is an energy greater than that which we know to be true. That energy is limitless and eternal, and it contains all the information about our many incarnations and our other multi-dimensional existences. It contains the records of all our intentions which created this particular incarnation, and what we hoped to gain from it. It holds the key to many of the existential questions your society has grappled with for centuries; the philosophical revelations that will occur will completely turn all previous beliefs on their head.

Now is not the time for this to occur. The stage must be set for change, and while this is certainly the case now in your civilization, much more will have to change before these precepts can be accepted by the big thinkers of your era. As with all new discoveries, there will be many who will dispute it and even ignore it as the whims of a deranged mind. But there will eventually be sufficient proof which is irrefutable.

It is at this point in the evolution of your civilization that the true shift in consciousness will occur. The current shift is merely a time of preparation for this ultimate realization about the true nature of yourselves as spiritual beings. While there are many who believe in this, it is a belief based solely on faith, either through religion or spirituality, and not one which can be proven. In fact, the scientific community has come up with all sorts of theories about the need for religion and spirituality as a personality trait, or one that is encouraged by an innate fear of death and the powerlessness this creates. While there is a certain amount of truth in the theories surrounding organized religion, the truth is that all people carry within them the memory of their origins as spirit. Some carry this memory more deeply than others, burying it on purpose out of fear. Still others feel the call of that memory as a profound knowing that they can never fully identify, and then there are those who come to a realization of this knowing which they term enlightenment.

The scientific discovery of the nature of the soul will revolutionize the way your world is structured, from the community level up to the highest forms of government and business. People in your world will have to consider that their ego-driven lives based on the desire to accumulate, impress and outdo no longer serves them once we admit that there is a part of us that is greater than those material gains.

Again, there will be those who will resist this idea at all costs, and who will continue in their old ways until the day they pass on from this world. But scores of people will become awakened through this knowledge, and will completely turn their lives around because of it.

Once people become awakened to the reality of the soul, they will begin to have a remembering of the sacredness of this life and the intentions set when they incarnated. They will become more mindful of their thoughts and actions, and will strive to become more aligned with their true purpose of living. Seekers will no longer be looking for the meaning of life; instead, they will be looking for a higher expression of their soul's purpose, and will begin to see the benefit to their emotional responses to life and their intuitive knowing when they are on the right path.

This is why it is the spiritual leaders and lightworkers who are the true revolutionaries of the New Age. Through their work, others will begin to understand themselves better and will find the courage and support they need to adjust to this new paradigm. No longer will the scientific community be seen to have all the answers, and no longer will the free thinkers and spiritual gurus be scoffed at as delusional or misguided. There will be created a new community of researchers who combine spirituality and science to create a more holistic view of the nature of reality and what it means to be human.

As your scientists and physicists begin to broaden the scope of their fields of study, they will begin to see a picture emerge of the complexities of life beyond anything they could have dreamed of in a laboratory. Within the many aspects of the human soul lies the secrets of the multi-dimensional universe; here can be found the hidden formulas of time/space travel and the solution to the limitations of exploring the far reaches of space without damaging the human physical system. Just as we have discovered, your researchers can tap into the flexibility of the human spiritual essence which can be projected through time and space to explore and visit other realms of existence. This travel will no longer be limited by the lifespan of the human body, nor by the dangers of prolonged space travel on the health of the human body. When only the spiritual essence of a living being is projected, that being can continue its life in a whole and complete way, leaving only a part of itself to wander about through time and space in a quite holistic way.

Once the mysteries of the human soul are explored, there will be great advances in the integration of mind-body-soul to form a complete and integrated system which honors all aspects of the human being. No longer will one aspect dominate over the others. The physical system will still be treated with reverence, but the spiritual and metaphysical aspects of the human will be seen to be equally as vital to the survival, success and well-being of humans as a whole and complete unit of life. This will cause huge shifts in the way you experience life, and the external world will no longer be seen as a form of limitation or conflict, as it will be understood that the soul can survive any challenge or limitation placed upon it by the rigors of life.

No longer will mankind think of itself as a mere cog in the wheel of life; you will instead understand that you are the Universe itself in human form, created out of the stuff of the stars and planets, no less than all of creation in one divine essence of spirit, soul and physical matter. Not only will this enhance the way your view yourself, you will be more likely to feel the kinship with all living things and their own soul essence.

You can see how vital these studies are in advancing the liberation of your species from some of the challenges which it is now facing. Understanding our own divinity is a key point in being motivated to save the aspects of your world which are under threat of annihilation.

As stated, the study of and integration of the mind-body-soul is an important part of understanding the true nature of human life, although there will be some who do not understand the aspects of this which do not conform with the traditional sense of scientific study. Therefore, there will be those who would deride this experimentation, as there are many skeptics who already denounce any kind of metaphysical study as being delusional and a waste of time. As we have stated previously, there will always be those who do not understand the need for change in any particular way of life, and so those who resist change will always find a reason to disengage from it.

However, one only needs to look at the natural way children are integrated with all aspects of their being to understand the true nature of life in all its aspects. A child is naturally inclined to express itself through all the aspects of its being. It will experience life in a physical sense, and as a young infant, will not be aware of its physical nature as being separate from that of any other physical sensation and connection it has. It will see its parents as a physical extension of itself, and will be unaware of any individual distinction between itself and the rest of the world. This is the natural sense of oneness which is still present within the soul of the child and which has not been tainted by a false sense of separation. This sense of personal identity develops at a later stage in the growth of the infant, and unfortunately, that sense of oneness is not usually recaptured.

The child will also experience the world through both the physical senses and the intuitive senses of feeling and awareness. Its awareness of its surroundings is based not just on its physical sensation, but also on its emotional sensitivity to energy. This intuition was developed in the womb and it is an important aspect to survival in the early stages of an infant's life when logical and intellectual thought is not yet fully developed. The child will have instincts for survival which include suckling, a startle reflex to a sense of danger, a grasping reflex to help it hold on when being carried, a cry to draw attention to its needs, and stimulation of its senses through the expression of love and caring shown to it. In these early stages of life, we are not in any way aware of a separation between these vital aspects of our relation with the world around us. Each sense is just as important as another, and in fact, we rely most heavily upon our inner senses in those early days than we do on our somewhat flawed physical senses.

Thus, many children experience intuitive and psychic sensitivities from an early age, connecting more closely with the energy of their surroundings and sensing the energy of spirit. It isn't until they are culturally conditioned to see that this is not an acceptable form of behavior that they will begin to turn this around to appear "normal." There are those children whose sensitivities have not only innocently predicted amazing events, but who have also conversed with spirit in a casual way and connected with a previous life in a very real and profound way.

These natural inclinations toward connecting with the energy field which surrounds you is often fully expressed by young children, only to be explained away as an active imagination or fantasy by well-meaning parents who do not wish to view their children as being anything other than normal. But many children experience this sensitivity in one form or another, and it is important that this phenomenon be studied so that a better understanding of what actually comes very naturally to us can be developed. Once the mainstream scientific community can come to grips with this very natural and real phenomenon, further advances can be made in the fields of physics and metaphysics which will allow for energetic work, leading to amazing progress in the fields of the study of the Universe, the human connection to All that Is, and the inner workings of consciousness.

This is the true domino effect of scientific advancement which can be realized in a fairly short amount of time, once the barriers to scientific inquiry are broken. These barriers are already beginning to be chipped away in the fields of quantum physics and certain integrated modes of thinking within the spiritual community. There will be much more to come from those who are looking to create this change to a more open-minded approach to scientific exploration. As you begin to recognize the interdependence of the mind-body-soul system, then the same concepts will be applied to the systems which are present in all life forms, including that of the entire Universe, down to the smallest insect colonies on your planet. Understanding the interconnectedness of all life will certainly cause a more liberal approach to the dissemination of assistance to those less fortunate than you, and the compassion gained through that feeling of oneness will certainly ease the suffering of those whose lives have been less than fortunate, and who are often shunned by community services with standards surrounding those they are able to serve.

It is most important for you to understand the ripple effect of not only your behavior and actions, but your thoughts and energy as well. As is taught by many spiritual masters, we are all made of energy, and all energy is responsive to the energy around it. This means that whenever you are connecting with another in any way, no matter how distant that connection is, your energy is having an effect on that person. The energy that you emit comes from your words, your actions, your physical state of being, your thoughts, your emotions and the focus of your attention. And so if you are distracted by stresses unrelated to the situation at hand, those stresses will be felt by the person you're connecting with and they will sense a feeling of unease and scattered focus. If you are focused on some negative situations in your life, that will be felt as well, both on a conscious level and on a deep, spiritual level.

This does not mean that you should at any time deny your feelings and try to suppress anything negative which you experience. It does, however, mean that you should be aware of how you're feeling, where your focus is and what type of energy you are emitting when you are dealing with certain delicate situations. For instance, if you are not in a positive frame of mind, it is probably not a good time to initiate a serious discussion with someone who is important to you. Even if you were to try to cover up your emotions, they would come through in your energy field and be felt on a certain level.

As a spiritual being within a human experience, it is vital that you acknowledge ALL aspects of this experience as sacred and divine, and that includes the times when you experience emotions that can be considered negative, such as anger, hatred, irritation, frustration, etc. These emotions are vital to the human experience, and they are part of the reason you decided to incarnate into this experience as a human being. The contrast offered by these emotions provide you with immense opportunities for growth and discovery through the choices you make in handling these emotions. If you allow these emotions to overtake you for long periods of time, some of these lessons will not be effected in that experience, but if you make healthier choices in dealing with these emotions in such a way that they foster growth and expansion, you'll find that they can greatly assist you as you move forward into a state of spiritual enlightenment, which is mainly about knowing oneself.

The energy that is emitted in an emotional state, either positive or negative, is very powerful. The emotions act as a conduit for your thoughts and feelings and so when you experience a negative emotion, the power and force behind that energy is very strong. It is important that you make it your intention to deal with these emotions as quickly as possible, without ignoring or negating them in any way, for the longer you leave them to fester and grow, the more difficult it is to see the deeper meaning behind them. Emotions that you wish to release must first be faced, acknowledged and seen as a real and palpable part of your life's experience. Then you must decide how long you are going to dwell in that space of negative energy so that you can then set the intention to move through the emotion and flip it to an energetic experience which feels more resonate with your peaceful center.

Once you are able to learn to master the emotional experience, you will find yourself dwelling in these darker places for shorter periods of time, and you will be able to bless these experiences as the highly sacred events which create strength, resiliency and compassion within you. You will also notice that others around you respond less negatively to you when you are working through difficult times, and will help to uplift and support you when you allow them to do this.

And so learning to master your emotional energy is vital not only to your own well-being and state of mind, but for the sake of those around you who are also affected by the energy your emit. The ripple effect of those who conduct themselves with the intention to spread peaceful and joyful energy more often than not is that others will feel the benefits of that which they will then pass on as they connect with others. And so you can see the immense power of just one kind word as you go about your daily life.

These kind acts cannot only be reserved for those who you feel are deserving of them. It is often those who you feel deserve them the least who are most in need of them, and again, not just for their own benefit, but for the benefit of all who will come into contact with them throughout their day. A single kind word or small act of kindness can have such a profoundly positive effect, it is quite like the butterfly effect in chaos theory which states that the single flap of a butterfly's wings can cause drastic changes in the weather on the other side of the globe. Your small words and deeds are much like that butterfly's wings; seemingly small and ineffective, but possessing great energetic power as the energy is passed throughout the system.

There are those whose energy is more connected with yours than others, such as family members and close friends, and you must realize that this energetic connection is not weakened by distance, nor is it severed by disagreements, inattention or time. These connections will last throughout your earthly life and beyond, and so your energy will forever affect the energy of those people forevermore. There are spiritual bonds which cannot be broken, no matter what the earthly experience presents to them, and any form of shift in these relationships can only serve to provide the opportunity for growth and understanding. Some ties are never broken, and some are temporary and short-lived, but all encounters are sacred and vital to the life experience that you have designed for yourself.

Never underestimate the power that a brief encounter can have on the workings of the universe. Every soul that passes through your energy field is altered in some way by your energy. It is part of the master plan of the universe that you experience this illusion of separateness, so that you can feel the essence of each other as different aspects of yourselves, and learn from the energy of these different aspects as they are shown to you in your daily experience. As such, every encounter provides you with the divine opportunity to see another aspect of yourself which you may have been previously unaware of. That includes those people who challenge you the most; look deep inside yourself and you will find that the very traits which most irritate and annoy you and even those which create strong feelings of repulsion or horror in others are reflected in yourself. We cannot escape some of the more negative aspects of ourselves, but we can always choose a different response to those aspects which will allow them to be experienced in a more positive way. This is one of our hardest lessons in an incarnated life; to bless every difficult situation for the wisdom it can offer us.

And so, as you can see, it is very important to your life's experience to always consider the energetic effect of your words, thoughts, actions and deeds, as these effects can be much more far reaching and important than they may be initially thought of on the surface. As we allow ourselves to be guided into right action, we will find that the encounters we have with others always afford us the opportunity to advance and grow. Sometimes these are hard lessons, but they are always valuable to our experience in this incarnation. Not one encounter, incident or life experience is without merit. You will often be totally unaware of the effect some small word or deed has had on another. Never take these encounters for granted, and remain mindful of your energy as you move through your day. You never know who it is going to affect.

Chapter Seven ~ The Nature of Animals

There have been great strides made in your civilization to increase the amount of respect and protection afforded to your animal kingdom. This increased sense of compassion and heart-centered connection with other creatures is one of the true signs of a positive shift in energy, leading from a sense of separation from other sentient beings to one of feeling connected and experiencing a kinship with all the living beings on your planet. In just a few short years, there have been many advancements in animal protection and a reduction in some cruel practices which victimized the animal kingdom and seemed to create a clear hierarchy, placing Mankind at the top and all other beings in a position of enslavement to the whims of Man.

In the last several decades, however, many have dedicated their time and lives to the awareness of cruel treatment among certain organizations and scientific laboratories. As the public outcry grows stronger, many of these practices are abandoned for other, less cruel ways of testing certain products and learning about medicines and drugs.

Understand that the treatment of animals is a strong indicator about the state of a civilization. If one is insensitive to the emotional and spiritual aspect of another sentient being, it is quite likely that this person will also be oblivious to the sacredness of life in general, and would not feel much respect for himself or other people. It is this state of unconsciousness which perpetuates cruel behavior, both toward animals and fellow human beings.

As the public makes it clear that cruel behavior will not be tolerated, other means of performing scientific enquiry are constantly being advanced, and other unsavory practices are becoming less acceptable in various businesses.

This comes as no surprise, as one of the greatest benefits of this current shift of consciousness is an increased sense of compassion and oneness, both with your fellow humans and with the animal kingdom. It stands to reason that most people who are advancing themselves spiritually also have a strong affinity for the animal kingdom. In order to truly feel self-love and respect, it is important that one feels respect, love and connection with all living beings.

There are many different ways to demonstrate your connection to the animal kingdom. Some will eschew all consumption of animal products as a sign of their connection with all other beings, while others will care for a pet with great love and devotion. Still others will rally and petition for stronger laws governing the treatment of animals, and some will work with animals in one form or another.

However, there are those who, while acting with the best intentions, will prefer animals over their fellow humans. This behavior only serves to further alienate them from that sense of oneness which is so important to an elevated spiritual life. If one can only find unconditional love in a connection with an animal, that person is truly missing out on the wonderful opportunities afforded us each day to rise above any doubts, judgment or hurt to love all others as we love ourselves. Our pets do not judge us, and if we would like to emulate this, it is important that we find it within ourselves to love all without judgment.

It is truly one of the reasons many of you are so drawn to the kingdom of pets and wild animals alike. It is their authenticity and innocence that is admired by these people. They see no pretense in an animal, though they will often point this out in humans. They feel no judgment or disappointment from animals, although they will often feel judged and disappointed by others.

There is some difference of opinion among scientists and animal-lovers over the nature of consciousness when it comes to animals. There are those who believe that animals are not capable of complex emotions and that their shows of affection are simply bids for attention. And there are those who truly believe that animals have the ability to communicate telepathically and understand their owners' emotions and feelings. It is certain that the emotional bond between humans and their pets can be quite strong, and that this emotional bond far transcends any lack of compassion or empathy on the animals' part.

White it is true that animals cannot experience some of the more complicated modes of thinking, they certainly can feel a large range of emotions and feelings, and that they are able to bond with humans and other animals in a real and affectionate way.

It is a mark of a compassionate society when people decide to keep pets. There is an aspect of unconditional love that one shares with an animal; it is a love based on nothing but the deep, abiding nature of oneness that one feels with a sentient being. There ensues a great need to protect and preserve animals among those who generally feel that sense of oneness with all beings of the earth, although there are some who feel more affection for the animal kingdom than they claim to feel for their human neighbors. This reluctance to feel the inner connection with fellow humans comes from a sense of expectation and "rightness" which one's ego can convince oneself is a fair and accurate judgment of others. In fact, this judgment tends to hold us in a place of separateness from not just the humans, but from all sentient beings, since we will focus our energy on being separate from the rest of the creation.

When one is able to remember one's connection to all living beings and the Universe in general, one will find herself becoming more gentle and kind with all living beings, and will not have the cloying sense of ownership which some will feel within it comes to an animal companion or a even a human family member. Those who are able to understand the spiritual nature of connection which binds us to all living things will be better able to view all others with a sense of compassion and understanding, rather than one of judgment and irritation.

Most pet owners would not scold or punish the cat who kills a small creature and brings it home to its owner, no matter how horrified that owner may be at the small gift. However, we will very swiftly turn to judgment and disgust when a fellow human does an act of cruelty or what we would consider "wrong" action. It seems so much easier to forgive an animal her transgressions rather than improving one's own condition with compassion, forgiveness and understanding, even when we are faced with very challenging situations.

An animal lover will love even those animals who refuse to take orders and perform on command, however, many will criticize those whom they believe are creating "wrong" scenarios and acting with cruelty or selfishness. It is important that we realize that directing the negative power of hatred, disgust and superiority only leads to much self-destructive behavior, as it creates a feeling of competition and self-righteousness which is unhealthy and contrary to the natural state of oneness that we feel when we are in our highest vibratory state. One cannot harmonize with oneself and the rest of humanity when one is judging and complaining about the behavior of another.

It has been scientifically proven that caring for a pet is enormously good for the health of a pet owner, and that the act of petting or playing with a pet can help improve the health of those who suffer with chronic complaints. Is this simply because the coat of most animals is soft and pleasing, or could it be something else?

We feel that the good feelings that ensue when one is in communion with an animal come from the primal sense of oneness that puts us in the best possible resonance with our higher selves and which helps us to feel closer to God. But understand that this feeling isn't necessarily relegated to one's experience with animals. It can come just as easily with another human being, even when you feel that this person is least deserving of your time, attention and love. It creates a high vibration, uplifted emotions and heightened awareness when we act in kind and compassionate ways toward everyone who comes into our lives.

The vast majority of people who have spiritual and psychic sensibilities also have an affinity to the animal kingdom and this is no coincidence. It is necessary for anyone on a spiritual path to cultivate compassion toward all living creatures and of course, to oneself. The affinity toward animals is just a reaching out of the soul in the spirit of oneness and connection, with no regard to that life form's species or belief system. This is the true meaning of unconditional love, understanding the importance of honoring all life forms in an equal way, and not favoring one just because of its usefulness to you or its physical appeal. We tend to look for those creatures which have cuddle appeal with soft coats and pleasant dispositions, but it is also important to see the importance of even the fly and the other ground-dwelling insects. In the natural world, these are crucial links to ourselves during the times when we were not sure where we belonged.

By feeling an affinity with the other creatures, we create a point of focus for our own physical presence on the earth. Having other life forms around us remind us that we are not alone and that there is still beauty and innocence around us. It gives us something to care about outside of ourselves, which makes us feel needed and valuable. It reminds us of what our lives are about and how we are part of a larger picture of life forms working in integration on a living organism which is the planet. When we can see ourselves as part of a system, this can keep us grounded and feeling more aligned with our purpose in this lifetime.

The animal kingdom is full of an incredible amount of diversity on your planet. It is one of the things that is so innately fascinating to those of us who originate from worlds with much less diverse species of sentient beings. Your animal kingdom is quite extraordinary among worlds, and so it is quite important that you treat it with respect, and honor it as an amazing part of your physical experience. It is true that this honoring of species has not always been an easy state of mind for many humans as they have been programmed by the culture to want to achieve dominion over all that is seen and all that could be cultivated for the new world order. This often included culling those species which have appeared to be in your way of development without regard for the necessity of that species to the circle of life. This has caused huge disparities on the rich diversity that once roamed your planet, although there is still such an amazing array of creatures that we have never experienced at any other time in our journeys.

In regards to those who mistreat or abuse animals, this indicates a missing component of compassion for the creature as a sentient being. In order for people to be able to kill or harm another creature, there must be some type of conditioning or programming present which makes that being less than important as a living organism to those who will decide its fate. Those who would abuse animals do so out of a sense of fear for their own dominion over the diversity of life on your planet. They will feel a certain amount of fear and trepidation when considering their role in the planet once the shift has fully occurred and it is realized that the old world order has disappeared. There is a sense of hopelessness around those who would harm another creature which stems from a sense of powerlessness. When one feels powerless over their own lives, they will seek to create a false sense of power through the assertion of their will over others in some way. It is true that those who would abuse an animal would be more likely to harm another person, as they lack the emotional component of true compassion which would preclude any ability to harm another creature.

Know that the souls of animals are whole and complete, and they survive the death of the physical just as humans do. They are often part of our original soul family who come into our lives during various lifetimes as our beloved pets, and they will often greet us joyfully when it is our time to cross over. This unbridled joy often eases us into the state of transition with a sense of peace and ecstatic reunion, helping us to realize our state of being as a spirit. Our animals serve vital purposes in our life paths, helping us to overcome some of the difficulties we face and giving us a grounded center, connected to our home planet and to others through the experience of love they provide. Caring for another being helps us to get out of our ego self and raises our vibration to a state of higher tranquility. They truly are gifts to our lives.

The animal kingdom has its own diverse array of emotions and methods of communication that, while to some may seem primitive, are actually quite advanced and complex. Never think that just because you cannot understand that communication that it is not occurring in a very real and structured way among most species of animals. There is a higher consciousness which is more readily available to these creatures whose limbic system does not allow for the sense of separation and egoic awareness that plagues the higher creatures. They are free from judgment and compassion, and are quite content in their own being. They take care of their needs and desires with no sense of guilt or pride, and they do not know cruelty, even though we will sometimes see some of their actions as cruel. There is great tenderness among the animals and a strong sense of community and affection. There is much that could be learned by observing and honoring them.

As you come to understand the nature of animals, it is inevitable that you will begin to also see yourself as a member of the animal kingdom and see your place among those creatures which you may deem below you in their state of consciousness. However, this is not necessarily the case. The elevated intellect of the sentient human does not necessarily mean that the spirit is also elevated. All living beings are equal in their sense of the soul being and their state of consciousness. There is not one being that is more divine than another, and the state of awareness that each creature exhibits has nothing to do with their spiritual state of being.

It is often wondered if animals reincarnate, and we would like you to know that they do, although on a different level than humans. Their life choices are made with less intention than that of humans, as their needs are not the same; however, they do have a life path which is similar to that of the human, and they will choose that life path to best put them in the situation to not only experience life from the vantage point of the creature consciousness, but also to have the greatest effect on those creatures around them. There is no life that is more or less valuable than another, but the creatures of your planet will accept their inevitable demise with the grace and dignity afforded a creature of such a spiritual awareness of consciousness.

While it is true that all animals have a built-in system of fear which is made to keep them alive in dangerous situations, this fear will rarely hold them back from the experiences of their lives as either wild or domestic creatures. The fear is made to keep them alive when faced with a predator or a dangerous situation, and that is exactly what it does. It is only the human being that will transmute their fear into something which holds them back from fully experiencing life.

When an animal faces death, its instincts will cause it to attempt to flee the situation, but when an animal meets death, it is with the peaceful surrender of a being who is one with its inevitable fate. Animals do not have the ego state which will create a sense of separateness from other creatures; therefore, it does not have the portion of the brain which allows it to perceive itself and separate and superior. To the animal, it just IS, without any need to judge, rationalize or create a sense of superiority. They are simply pure love and joy, and they will find great contentment with a peaceful sense of themselves and their place in the Universe.

Chapter Eight ~ Spirits Among You

We have described to you previously the nature of ourselves as spirit beings, but not in the conventional sense of spirit which you may be used to. While we are conversing as spirit beings, we have not passed on to the spiritual plane as those do whose lives have come to an end; however, we are able to commune with those types of spirit beings and as such, we have gained valuable knowledge about the nature of the afterlife. We also have knowledge about the different types of spirit beings and their roles in the lives of incarnated souls such as yourself.

As discussed previously, the soul transitions at the time of the death of the body into a clear, pure aspect of being. These transitioned souls exist as a form of energy which, while closer to the essence of the souls' true form, still maintain some aspects of the life it just passed away from. The aspects of this spirit being include all the experiences and lessons from the life it just left, and it retains all the memories of that life as though it were still an incarnate being. This is the essence of the soul which is tapped into by mediums such as this channel, and this is why these spirit beings can be identified through the recognizable physical and personality traits which they exhibited in life.

It is important to remember, however, that this aspect of the soul is not all there is to a complete and organic soul being, as the soul is multi-dimensional and contains the aspects of many different incarnations throughout many different lifetimes and many different dimensional existences. So the spirit with which you communicate in a mediumship reading is only the aspect of that soul which you knew in life. As this spirit transitions through the many different phases of existence in what you call the afterlife, this earthly aspect will begin to fade, although the memories and lessons from the life will remain. It is still possible to tap into this earthly aspect of the soul, however, as it still exists in a certain dimensional plane; however, the true integrated soul will begin to lose those aspects of the earthly personality over time.

This, of course, describes the transition of spirit which occurs in a traditional sense, and this is what is experienced by the vast majority of spirits in the process of death and ascension. There are those, however, who do not experience this transition fully, and these spirits may become lodged in a state of attachment to their earthly incarnation despite having lost the physical nature of that incarnation. These spirits are what is known as the earthbounds, and they often make themselves known as ghosts to those in the physical. There are many reasons for this to occur, and while it may sometimes seem to be a cruel fate, please be assured that these spirits are always being cared for, although in some cases they are unaware of this care and guidance and persist in their state of confusion. No spirit will be stuck in this phase forever, and again, understand that this is only one aspect of the whole that is in this state of limbo; the true soul which is attached to this spirit continues on its path in the etheric realm.

These spirits can sometimes appear angry and dangerous, and it is true that their energetic composition will retain the emotions of the life that they lived, and these emotions can sometimes drive them to create disturbances for the humans around them. It is quite rare, however, that any real harm could be done, but it is best not to try to provoke those spirits who are exhibiting signs of disturbed or violent behavior, just as you wouldn't provoke any living person with these characteristics. Know that whatever experiences they are having in this static state are part of the soul's ascension and they will eventually pass through this phase of their transition.

There are many other types of beings which exist in the realm of spirit, most of which have not incarnated into a physical existence. These include those which you define as angels. These beings are energy in its purest form, multi-dimensional and unlimited in their scope. They are the guardians and protectors of both those on earth and those in the spirit realms. They will sometimes show themselves to those who need to see them, and this vision will often be one of the traditional form of an angel, with wings and a glowing light. Understand that this is only for the benefit of those who are viewing this apparition, so that they are able to identify what they see. The true form of angelic energy is not in any way related to the human form, although it can transmute into any form which is required for the task at hand.

These angelic beings serve to guide and protect those who are in need of assistance during certain trials and challenges in their existences. They will intervene in the lives of incarnate souls when asked, and they will gently guide through subtle signs and signals when needed. There are scores of these beings in existence, and each is able to exist in many different forms and in many different dimensional spaces at one time, and so the scope and power of these beings is unlimited. As such, when you call upon the guidance of angels, you can be sure that it always responds. The archangels that you have been taught about are quite real, but they are not quite as defined as you may think and their power is not relegated by rank or hierarchy. There are some which do possess supreme power, which could fall under the auspices of archangel, but all angels, even those which you may consider lesser, posses great power and unlimited love.

Other beings which populate the unseen realms include what you consider the elemental spirits, or the spirits of nature. These beings are part of the natural world, just as vital to it as its plant life and animals. They can be quite protective of their habitat, and as such, are sometimes seen as mischievous, but understand that their role is one of guardianship and stewardship of the land. They are pure energy and light, although they can be seen as various mythical creatures as the brain interprets that energy and light into something which is more familiar to it. As such, fairy energy will sometimes been seen as small, winged creatures, since this pleases the energy of those beings and the human mind is able to process that image as something it can relate to. The same can be said for woodland elves and gnomes; this energy is of a lower vibration, and so is often interpreted as small, human-like creatures which are low to the ground. Again, these creatures are pure energy which can manifest itself in a visual way through the process of the visual cortex and relatable memory.

It is important that you understand that while the vast majority of these energetic beings exist in the light, there are also beings which exist in the lowest vibrational aspects. These beings are what you often regard as demons or devils, and their energy is a direct contrast to that of the light beings we have already discussed. This energy is a direct reflection of those aspects of every incarnated being which can serve to attract that energy and allow it to flourish. This is a very complex process, and the nature of these beings is much too difficult to describe in a short work; however, understand that there is a direct correlation between the aspects of dark energy and those aspects which exist in all incarnated beings. Most beings are able to suppress this darkness through love; however, as you see in your society, some cannot, and the darkness overwhelms them. This is not a pleasant energy to deal with, but it is not insurmountable. Dwelling with this energy is a choice, as is dispelling it through the light of love and compassion.

And so, understand that to dwell in a place of fear is to create a lower vibration which could possibly resonate with that of the darker energies, thus creating that which is being feared. It is quite true that only the light can drive out the darkness, and so the best way to conquer any fear of dark energy both within and without, is to dwell in a place of love, compassion and kindness, which lifts the vibration and therefore rises above any of the lower vibrational energetic beings.

All of these beings can be seen as reflections and aspects of the incarnate, and as multi-dimensional energetic life forms, you all possess various aspects of these beings within you. You are not often aware of these energetic aspects as you are preoccupied with the physical, but when you are in certain states of consciousness and in certain vibrational alignments, you may experience a connection with these beings as they reflect and represent these aspects within yourself. As such, an angelic presence appears not just to lift you up when you are weak, but to remind you that you possess the same strength within you. The elemental spirits reflect your connection to the Earth and its material aspects, and the lower energies are manifestations of the darker forces which provide the contrast and challenge needed to exercise free will.

There is much fear surrounding some of these entities, and this fear can greatly alter the experience of perceiving the energetic elements of them. Fear is always associated with the unknown and the unexplained, and so if someone perceives an unfamiliar energy around them, the body will set up a chain reaction of chemical responses which will lead to a physical shift of awareness. This shift can greatly alter the perception of the person who is experiencing this energy and it can then be interpreted in such a way as to support this fear. For instance, if a person senses the energy of a spirit nearby and has a fearful reaction to this, the physical and chemical reaction to that fear can alter the senses to such a degree that the experience matches the fearful expectation. This does not mean that the person is imagining the entire experience, only that their interpretation of the experience may not be reliable when it is perceived through the lens of fear.

Also, it is important to understand that the state of mind of a person can also have an effect on their ability to perceive and correctly interpret the energy of the unseen world. If someone is experiencing great stress, or some mental instability, their perceptions are most likely to be altered, and as such, their reaction to an experience may not be completely in line with the real truth of that experience. As such, a grieving person may not be completely at ease with the experience of their loved one's energy around them, and so they will most likely block out any perception of that energy, or they will simply feel uneasy and sad in reaction to the reminder of the person who was lost. They will often feel uncomfortable but not know why, chalking it up to the emotions of grief that they are experiencing.

If you wish to commune with the spirit of lost loved ones, it is most important that you enter into this pursuit with a level of calmness, acceptance and few expectations. This will allow your consciousness to relax and accept the experience without fear or expectation of what the spirit may say or do. The greater the allowance, the more likely it will be that the spirit will find a way to communicate.

Understand that energetic beings interact with the energies of the planet, and that these energies can also have an effect on the way that these entities manifest in the material world. This is why most spirit encounters occur in the nighttime hours, as the energy in the atmosphere shifts in darkness with the moisture in the air and the radiating heat from the cooling Earth, combined with the cooler air of the night. While spirit is able to manifest during the day, they are more easily perceived at night, and their energy may be a bit more powerful in the nighttime conditions.

There is some debate over the anomaly of orbs appearing in photographs. The research that has been done indicates a certain amount of conscious behavior of these orbs and so there are some who theorize that these orbs are manifestations of spirit energy. This is true, and it is a conscious manipulation of spirit energy which is able to create this visible evidence of their presence. The orb itself does not contain the energy of the spirit; rather, the spirit is able to manipulate the surrounding energy to such an extent that that manipulation is displayed in the natural shape of an orb which is evidence of the presence of spirit. These orbs will often appear in strategic places in the photographs of those who experience them, and they are sometimes so bright that there is no mistaking them for dust or moisture anomalies. This is a very real and accurate occurrence which could do with a bit more serious study, as so far, this phenomenon is often looked upon with disdain as a false or deceptive practice.

Spirits want you to know they are there. They want to give you the comfort of knowing that they have not left, that life is eternal, and that their love still exists in the annals of time and space. They also want you to understand yourself as spirit, since this understanding can completely change a person's outlook on their lives. If you were to truly understand the nature of your being, you would rarely have an anxious or stressful moment, because you would know that as a divine creature, the world is actually at your feet. There is no spirit energy which can badly harm or take things away from you, although again, those who delve in the darker energies will need to be ready to deal with the consequences of opening their energy to those forces. Those who dwell in the light rarely call in anything that is not of the light, as all experiences with spirit will mirror what the individual is feeling inside, just as experiences with other humans and life circumstances will always mirror that which the person is believing about themselves and the world. And so if you experience a negative spirit encounter, it is important that you look within yourself to understand what it is that may be attracting such energy into your life.

As you can see, there are many different forms of energy present at any given moment. We have dealt with only a few of these energy forms, but understand that there are countless beings in existence who dwell in other dimensional realities and in the vast richness of space. While all of these life forms share a common denominator, which is that they are, at their true essence, soul beings, the variety of physical manifestations of these beings is unlimited in scope. The human race would do well to remember that they have only just begun to scratch the surface when it comes to the exploration of consciousness, dimensional reality and space exploration, and that the truth of the existence of other life forms and energetic beings is far beyond what anyone could fathom.

Chapter Nine ~ Dialogue with Frank

Questions and Answers

L.L. asks: Frank, do you know of the entities that call themselves Abraham from Abraham-Hicks? If so, how are you the same/different? What is the easiest way for humans to connect with spirit? Do you have any tips for someone with an "ADD" type brain to be able to more easily get and stay focused on a task/goal/thought, etc.? Thank you!

We are aware of the entity group known as Abraham and the extensive work they have done through their channel, Esther Hicks. This group of entities has come forth for very similar purposes to those of our own, and their work is to be commended. Know that their time spent on this work is limited, but that their written work will stand the test of time. There are many lessons to be learned and the teachings of Abraham will always be an important work to refer to as your planet continues on its energetic shift.

This group of entities bears some similarities to our energy but we are not one and the same in the way you define it. They are a group of light beings; that is, they are from a dimensional space which is separate from that of this Universe, but as with all dimensional spaces, they are closely connected to this one. They are purely energetic beings, and are not incarnate at this time, although they have been in some type of physical existence at some point which is why they can so clearly relate their teachings to the minds and attitudes of incarnate humans.

The easiest way for humans to interact with spirit is to simply allow it to occur. This sounds much easier than it really is, because of the deeply-held beliefs and fears surrounding spirit communication and death. If one is able to create a sense of safety and protection which will largely eliminate fear, drop any expectations of what will be experienced with this spirit communication, and ask for the highest form of connection while in a very relaxed and receptive state, it is quite likely that some form of communication will occur. In fact, spirit often communicates with their loved ones but often these forms of communication are shrugged off as simply tricks of the mind or fantasy. In order to truly experience a higher connection, one must closely examine any deeply-held beliefs and fears that will potentially block any form of spirit communication.

As for advice about how to overcome a deficit in attention, it is important to examine how these types of labels can create the mind and body to react in such a way that the diagnosis becomes part of the reality of the subject. In other words, we become what others declare that we are, if we allow ourselves to be drawn into the energy of that diagnosis and we accept it as our reality. While there appears to be an epidemic of humans with attention deficit disorders and behaviors which indicate that the individual is on the autism spectrum, these diagnoses are not always accurate. The shifting energy on your planet is bound to affect each person in a profound and unique way, and for some, it can cause disruptions in their ability to concentrate and focus on the world around them. This is because the shifting energy is pulling the vibration higher, and so the body reacts with certain chemicals which disrupt the cognitive abilities of the brain. The resulting difficulties in daily functioning can cause challenges for those individuals, and so they seek medical attention. Since it is the job of the medical professionals to give a concrete label to any seeming malady, and treat it with chemicals meant to correct the problem, the diagnosis of ADD or ADHD is simply being more widely given to those with varying degrees of this challenge. In short, if you believe this is a true diagnosis and you buy into the belief that this is who you are, it will be quite difficult to shift that reality.

Learning to focus and direct one's attention is a skill that can be difficult to master in a fast-paced society, but it is not impossible, even for those who have received these diagnoses. Just like any other change you wish to instill in your life, it require intention, challenging the habitual way you live your life, and repeated exercises to create a new pattern of perception and new neural pathways in the brain. We would recommend spending at least one or two hours a day in a completely focused pursuit which includes meditation, reading out loud, brain-exercising puzzles such as working with mazes and shapes, and grounding oneself by being out in nature. Just as it's possible to heal the body from any number of diseases or injuries, it is possible to heal the mind from the constant barrage of energetic, visual, auditory and sensory information which can confuse the brain and send it into a state of chaos. Also remember that many children being born in the last several decades are part of the evolutionary progression of cognitive function and spiritual awareness, and as such, they may have difficulty with the status quo when it comes to education and cultural norms. This does not mean that there is something in them that has malfunctioned; it means that the dysfunctional systems they are struggling with are about to change.

C.R. asks: Frank, I have a blue jay that sits outside my bedroom window every morning at the same time. He is quite loud and vocal. Can you tell me why and the message he delivers?

Yes, this blue jay is quite a happy fellow and he is receiving some influence from your father's spirit to greet you with his raucous calls. There is a sense that you believe your father has not communicated with you since his passing, but the blue jay is his method of choice to give you a loud and clear message which you cannot ignore, but which you can choose to attribute to simply a noisy bird or something which means more to you. See what happens when you acknowledge the blue jay's antics as coming through the energy of your father and pay attention to any shifts that occur when you address your father through the jay.

D.S. asks: Frank, every morning I wake up and hear the words, "Do you love me?" This is the deepest mystery of my life. I wonder who is asking whether I love them? Do I know them? What should I do if I do love them? What should I do if I don't love them?

D, as you come into the consciousness of awareness from the altered state of sleep, it is possible for your Higher Self, or the spirit at the essence of your being to communicate with you, and that is where this voice is coming from. There is an aspect of your current incarnation which is to assist you in the lessons of self-love, self-preservation and self-confidence which were sorely lacking in a previous incarnation. As such, your Higher Self wishes to remind you daily to focus on these aspects which will help you to go forward with greater faith in the callings of your heart and the wisdom of your soul. Self-love is essential for the work that you wish to do in this life, and this question not only asks you to reflect on this, but it is also asking what you are going to do in the coming day to demonstrate that love.

A.H. asks: How can we explain hauntings, demons, and possessions that require exorcisms?

As we explained in the previous chapter, there are many different types of energetic beings in your dimensional reality and even more in the alternate dimensions. There are many ways that these beings interact with the energy of incarnate beings, and these experiences are also very much influenced by the beliefs and fears of the people who are the subjects of these experiences. This does not in any way mean that their experiences are not real, it is simply important to recognize the responsibility of each individual for the energy they bring to any experience.

That which is called a haunting can be the result of a spirit who is existing in a state of reality which is not fully transitioned but is no longer attached to the physical realm. Some of these spirit beings experience anger, hostility, mental disorders or psychological which are carried over from their earthly existence into their experience as spirit. Understand that this state of turmoil is part of this spirit's experience of existence which has a purpose for the elevation of their highest soul being, and that they will eventually cross the threshold from one that is bound to the incarnated life they have left to their true spiritual home. Again, this aspect of the person is only a small part of their true soul existence. While it is sometimes the case that these beings interfere with the lives of those they encounter, it is most unlikely that they will do anything more than frighten or intimidate those people. Again, it is important to examine what it is about one's own energy which may be attracting such an experience into one's life, and to exert influence over these disincarnate beings by telling them they are not allowed to interfere with the lives of the people around them.

As for demonic energy and possession, it is true that there are lower vibrational energies which exist and can attempt to have an influence over incarnate beings, but it is a very rare occurrence and often something appearing to be a possession is actually an energetic disturbance within the individual. The exorcism will work because the individual believes that it will, just as the possession will appear genuine and unexplainable events will occur because the individual, and those around the individual, will believe that it is real. Understand that these beliefs and fears can attract the lower-lying energies which will add to the experience, but there is no energy known to existence which is all-powerful or able to manipulate the will of any being without some type of consent. That which is experienced as dark, malevolent and demonic energy MOSTLY exists within the energy of the individual, and is manifested externally. The original low-vibrational energy is much less powerful without the augmented energy of belief and directed focus.

R.P. asks: I have only in the last few years given much thought to "energy bodies" outside of the human. I always believed in them but did not try to define them or understand them, mainly until my experiences through you (Tracy) and your Spirit Galleries and channeling of Frank. So how would you describe the differences and similarities of earthbounds, ghosts, crossed-overs, spirits, angels, and group/other-worldly entitles like Frank? Thank you, Tracy and Frank.

Energy is energy, and the only thing that really differentiates the various forms of energy is frequency. While all energy retains a certain level of consciousness, lower-vibrating energy displays very little consciousness in the traditional sense and higher-frequency vibrations have the highest level of consciousness. And so, all beings in the physical world are somewhat limited in their vibration by the constraints of the physical body and the material world, including the forces of gravity and the limitations of physical location and movement. Once the spirit is freed from the body, either through astral travel or death, the vibration of the spirit is raised to the level of pure energy with no physical or material attributes, thus removing the limitations of the material plane.

When we consider the different levels of vibrational consciousness among different spirit beings, these also can be differentiated by frequency and consciousness. Thus, the lower-lying energies which vibrate at a lower frequency will be experienced as a heavy or dense energy, without much awareness or consciousness in their actions. These would be what would be called dark or demonic energy by some. Then there are the earthbound energies, which are the same as ghosts. These energies possess a vibrational state which is similar to that of an incarnated being, since they are somehow still attached to the physical life they have left, even though they no longer reside in a physical state. Because the frequency of these energy beings is so similar to that of humans, their movements and manipulations of the material world are more easily discerned by those on the physical plane and as such, these beings are seen as frightening and negative. As stated previously, this is not necessarily the case, and the disturbances created by these beings are normally a simple cry for attention.

Spirit who have completed their transition from the earthly plane to that of spirit have a higher frequency, and therefore are not easily detected. This higher frequency takes them to a different level of existence while still allowing them the opportunity to connect with those they have left behind in the physical plane. These connections will be quite subtle, however, and are sometimes not recognized by their loved ones, although on a deep soul level, they are aware of them.

Higher vibrational frequencies are found in other etheric beings such as angels, guides and masters. These beings have frequencies which transcend that of any human spirit. While some guides and masters will have had incarnated lives, most angels have not, and so they possess some of the highest frequencies in the etheric realm. This frequency allows them to intervene with the lives of incarnate beings while still maintaining a certain cloak of illusion. There are those who have had encounters with those whom they have believed to be human, but have questioned this fact as the being appears to disappear after offering some help or advice. Angels are able to manipulate energy to make themselves appear human when this is needed, and they are able to exert influence on the physical plane without being overtly detected.

While there is no hierarchy among spirit beings, there are many different levels of frequency which determine the power and scope of these beings; as such, these beings will be experienced in widely varying ways by humans. Again, it is important to consider one's own state of mind when calling upon any being in the spirit realm, as one's own frequency will have an influence on what type of energy is attracted.

The highest frequency of energy is, of course, that of the Supreme Intelligence, The Universe, or God. This energy far transcends any other frequency available in the realm of spirit, and it is this supreme vibration of love which is at the center of the spirit realm. As the frequency of spirit beings rises through intention, learning and experience, they come closer to this highest frequency, and it is possible that eventually they would merge with it if they so choose.

E. P. asks: What is the most important thing that each of us can do individually to help bring about peace, balance and the shift of consciousness?

The shift of consciousness is occurring naturally right now in the sphere of Earth's energy, and so the best way to work with this shift and take advantage of what it has to offer you is to continue to do the work which raises your own vibration in joy and peace. As you raise your frequency, you allow yourself to match the newer frequencies which are coming into your field of consciousness. The best way to work with your energy on an individual level is to make sure you are taking care of yourself energetically, physically, mentally and emotionally. When there is a balance among these aspects of the physical being, the frequency is raised and the individual is better able to match the rising frequencies of the shifting consciousness.

Bringing about peace and balance in one's external reality require that one must first develop these things internally. It is not possible to initiate external change without first making these changes internally, and so the first step is always to look at one's own life and state of consciousness. Practices such as meditation, mindfulness, kindness, compassion, and acts of love all serve to create a peaceful center which best attunes to the vibration of the higher self. When one is maintaining a higher frequency, they are better able to influence the energy of others around them without much effort. But if one's vibrational frequency is lowered by dwelling on the negative aspects of life, judging others, deliberately hurting or denigrating others, and disrespecting themselves, their influence will only be a negative one, if in fact they have any influence at all. Understand that the frequency of your vibration is heavily influenced by the decisions you make, and that these frequencies are in turn felt by those around you. And so your largest influence on the world is that which is initiated within through your most intimate thoughts and beliefs about the world, and the way that you go about your daily life.

Cultivating peace requires a certain amount of detachment, which may seem at odds with the idea of compassion. However, one is able to treat all others with much compassion and caring while still honoring their own life's paths. When one is at peace with oneself, it is clear to them that they are not attached to anything around them, as all things are transient and independent in one way, and immortal and connected in another. This may seem like a paradox to you, but as you practice detached compassion, confident caring and love without judgment, you will understand these concepts.

Understand that the greatest gift you have to give to the world is yourself. You are endowed with many gifts which you may choose to share or hide in this lifetime. Should you choose to share your heart's passions, you will have a tremendous effect on the energy of those around you and the energy of the world in general. Find your peace through doing your heart's work, spreading love and loving the divine which resides within you.

C. K. B. asks: Frank, whenever I find money on the ground, or see the numbers 22 or 222, I think it is the angels or guides telling me I am on the right path, or that thing I was just thinking or doing is putting me on the right path. Is this true? And, how do we know the difference between when we are making up stuff in our heads, as opposed to getting real guidance from our angels and guides?

We are given signs in many different ways from higher beings, and some of these signs include those things that are placed in your path or number sequences and music heard on the radio. Spirit and higher beings have ways of manipulating energy so that these things will appear to you as though they were just left there by someone else, when, in fact, they were placed there by an unseen hand, or someone was manipulated into leaving those things at that particular spot so that you can find them.

When you find money on the ground, it is a reminder that abundance is all around you at all times, and you simply need to reach out and grab it. There is a tendency for you to focus on that which you do not have, or what you gave up. It's vitally important that you focus on the ease and flow in your life, and when you find money, it gives you the sense of that ease and flow. As long as you can understand your role in the appearance of these gifts, you will find them coming more and more, as all of the Universe is involved in providing you with this reminder.

J. S. asks: Greetings, Frank! Thank you for sharing your love and wisdom through Tracy. I am wondering about emotions. I have believed for some time that to release any emotion that overwhelms us, whether it is one we consider "good" or "bad", all we have to do is feel the feeling fully, experience it entirely, and then it will dissipate. I also use EFT to release them from deep in our energy systems. But I find they do not release until we have felt them as much as our souls/higher selves want/need us to. The reason I think this is true is because we came as humans to experience feelings, to expand the universe's experience by feeling everything. And as we have feelings, new levels of being are created. So when people tell me they are afraid of something (and many of the things are pretty reasonable to incite fear in humans!), I teach (and practice myself) the idea that I need to see the worst case scenario of the fear, feel the feeling it creates in me, follow it through my body and then let it dissipate to peace. For me and many of my clients, this has brought great relief and new approaches to life. BUT I'm wondering if I have the whole story. I feel like I'm missing part of the puzzle and it's a really beautiful, fun piece. Can you help me figure this out? Thank you!

While you are correct in your premise that all emotions are to be experienced in the incarnated state, and that it is necessary to move through an emotional state in order to fully process it and learn from it, we do feel that these emotional shifts are best dealt with as they naturally occur; that is, as they arise as reactions to events and people which have an effect on our lives. To anticipate a negative emotion is not necessarily the best way to move through the emotional experience, since it is an imagined state of response rather than a natural one. If one is in a state of anticipated emotion, one is not fully absorbed in the feeling of that state, and is more likely to create unnecessary effects from the negative emotional state. These effects can be anything from simple anxiety and fear to deep scars on the psyche caused by the reaction to a perceived incident or threat. There are more than enough emotional lessons to be dealt with through the incidents and events of everyday life, and so moving through perceived or anticipated emotions is creating something which does not really exist, and as such, the person is not truly moving through and learning from the emotional state. They are simply using this fabricated response as a form of contrast with the peaceful state, thereby finding satisfaction in the contrasted state of peace. There is an element of falsehood here which is not really matching the genuine emotional experience.

It seems to us that a more productive form of emotional release is to deal with those emotions which have already occurred in the subject's life, and which they have difficulty releasing. If one is feeling blocked by fear, it is best to deal with that emotion of fear, rather than fabricating the possible emotional reactions to the incident they are fearing. While it may seem like a preventative measure to take a subject through every worst-case scenario in their minds, it is impossible to imagine every possible thing that could go wrong, and in fact, spending time fabricating negative fantasies does not create a positive, healing space in which the subject may experience true healing. It is causing a feeling of anticipated pain and suffering, and even if the subject appears to be more relaxed and accepting of these experiences, the subject will, in the long run, be more likely to be confused and unsure of their true emotions.

There is much to be learned and benefited from one who faces, acknowledges, expresses and moves through an emotional experience, and there are certainly times when assistance is needed to help someone release emotions that have not been fully expressed. However, it is important that these are based on the person's truth, their real experiences, and their genuine reactions to life events, and not fabricated in the mind as a form of anticipated release. This carries a level of falsehood which can be misleading and confusing, even though the subject feels a sense of relief afterward. If there is to be an element of fantasy in the emotional release, let it be one in which the subject imagines the best possible outcome, rather than the worst.

J. K. asks: Frank, everyone on earth seems so preoccupied with the physical world, understandably so. But what needs to happen for the people of the world to pay more attention to their higher selves and the spirit around them? How can we make that shift?

The shift in consciousness in your world is one that is naturally occurring at the present time. There will be those who will be deeply affected by this shift, and who may change their stance from one of doubt and skepticism to one of self-awareness and spiritual awakening. But there will be still others who will appear to have no discernible changes in their minds and lives through this shift, and this is just as important as those who do experience a change. This is because the contrast will be needed going forward to add validity to the need for change and to demonstrate the difference that these varying levels of consciousness have on the person's spiritual state, mental state and levels of satisfaction with life.

Understand that it is never your responsibility to bring anyone into a state of spiritual awareness. This is something that can only be accomplished by the individual, although often this desire is sparked by some incident or observation about another person in his/her life. A person has to be in a particular state of mind in order to be willing to do what it takes to initiate this shift in consciousness, and so you will find may people in your life who are not in any way ready to experience the changes that are being offered to them. We must learn to let them be, and accept that their path is not one of spiritual growth in this lifetime.

The evolution of consciousness is a very personal experience, although it is also one very much guided by the collective consciousness. We must learn to allow each individual to experience their lives just as they see fit, and in a way which truly resonates with then. This means that you will find many people in varying degrees of spiritual awakening, and you will also find many who have little or no desire to improve, become more at peace with their own divinity, and who have little or no compassion for others. Let them be; they have much to teach us.

A, G. asks: Are humans capable of instant manifestation? If so, any tips on making that a reality in my life? Do beings/energies/collectives in other dimensions ever tap into human beings for information/answers? Always wondered if channeling is a two way street of asking and answers or if humans are just so low we need help from everyone else.

Yes, instant manifestation is possible to achieve and it has been experienced by some; however, it is a rare occurrence because it requires a level of detachment which is simultaneous with a state of heightened anticipation, joy and high vibrational awareness. This is not a state which is easily attainable by the masses, and so you will find that as you move through the process of manifestation, you are revealing that which has previously blocked your attempts to achieve the state that you desire. In other words, there are many hidden blockages to your ability to manifest the things that you want, not the least of which is self-doubt, the feeling of lack which accompanies a desire, a lack of confidence in one's ability to manifest, and an absence of the feeling of being deserving of those things. And so the answer is that this is absolutely an attainable goal, but it is one that is not easily achieved in your culture with its many influences which challenge the feelings of self-worth and deservedness in the vast majority of people.

Your second question can be answered with a resounding YES, as there are many who study humans and tap into their consciousness for wisdom and insight into the ways of handling challenge, defeat and cultural influence. There are a vast number of civilizations in the dimensional space your planet occupies, and many of these civilizations require some assistance with their daily lives. These beings will often tap into the consciousness of the human experience to obtain wisdom which can help them on their path to a higher spiritual plane.

Understand, though, that your Earth is different from any other habitable planet. We are, and others are, too, in great awe of the many achievements and advances your civilization has obtained in such a short amount of time. This level of accelerated evolution in the form of technology and lifestyle is unprecedented among local civilizations, and that is why other worlds are so eager to study and document your state of mind and your responses to the many challenges you now face.

C. H. asks: Frank, are there such things as demons? Are there beings actively working to bring destruction to humans or are we the victims of our exclusive co-creation of evil?

The lower vibrational energy which you call demonic does in fact exist in a state of consciousness which is not much different from your own. It is important to recognize that all states of consciousness exist in each other, and that it is only that state within which you place most of your energy that will take precedence in your life.

This lower vibrational energy is one which has been manifested by the human consciousness; that is, it cannot exist without its equivalent human form. This is true of all levels of consciousness experienced in your realm, as they are all part of one singularity. As such, this demonic energy of which you speak can only be brought into being by a vibrational match of some sort. It can be experienced at some level by those who are not entirely a vibrational match, but it cannot manifest in its true energetic form without being invited by some level of vibrational equivalent in human form.

Therefore, one who invites dark energies in through their intentions will often find success in this endeavor, and those who do so on a deeper level of consciousness will also find this energy being drawn into their lives. One whose intention is solely to connect with higher vibrational beings will be less likely to experience the lower-lying energies of so-called demons and other entities of this nature.

As all consciousness is one, all levels of vibration exist as one being at some level. Therefore, these lower energies are simply manifestations of that which already exists within all humans. The choice of whether to connect with them, and therefore bring them fully into existence, lies within each individual.

F. D. asks: Can you tell me if our (B.'s and mine) idea to split our lives between Sedona and NJ is sound and for the greater good? And we ask that you help us know the right time to do it.

We are quite aware of the struggles and challenges you have both been facing, and it is with delight that we observe that the manifestation of your true desires is beginning to unfold. There is a sense of movement in your path at the present time which is propelling you into a future of heightened service and deeper connection with those who will most benefit from the spiritual services you are providing. This connection will evolve as you move into a less permanent state of residence and find that your energy can be divided between the east and western regions of the country. Therefore, it is quite likely that you will find yourselves in the area of Sedona more and more often as you go forward, although it is not necessarily a permanent place of residence for you at this present time. There is still work to be done in the area where you currently reside, and the coming move will serve to free up some of your energy so that it can be better spent in service and in the planning of those events and audiences with those who will be touched by the compassionate service you extend.

There is nothing to fear at this time as all is in order for you to achieve all that you wish to experience in the remainder of your lives. It is without a doubt that we predict your success and fulfillment in all the endeavors you continue to undertake going forward. We are mightily impressed with all that you do and all that you give to the world in which you live.

D. P. asks: Will the Earth experience climate shifts in the near future due to increased solar activity?

The shifts in solar energy which are evident at this time can cause some energetic shifts in your atmosphere, and these are already occurring. Your weather patterns are cyclical, and while it may appear that there are climate shifts associated with the solar activity which is being measured in your current conditions, these weather patterns are quite independent of what is being experienced on the surface of the sun at this time.

It is more likely that the solar activity will create magnetic and gravitational shifts in your atmosphere which will have a deeper energetic effect on the planet and its inhabitants, rather than a climate effect, although this is something which will be attributed to it by some scientists. Your climate is more sensitive to cycles of shifts in pressure and the presence of debris in the atmosphere. These shifts are not new, and your Earth has always experienced cycles of climate change, and has always survived these shifts.

Solar activity is more likely to interfere with the magnetic fields governing electronic transmissions than it is your weather. However, there is also the matter of energetic shifts which effect the energy of consciousness, and so the solar shifts play a small part in the shift which is currently occurring on your planet. This influence is mostly a gravitational one, and although that shift is very subtle, its effects are not. However, rather than being a precursor to the end of your planet, it is part of the shift which is causing the spiritual awakening among you. It is precisely this awakening which will serve to save, not destroy, your world.

Made in the USA
Lexington, KY
02 July 2015